Food and health: Why the poor are sick and how to avoid it

A sociology of food, conscious of the links between food and health

Louis Lebredonchel

ISBN : 979-8878643320

Louis Lebredonchel, Bureau SH105, Maison de la recherche en sciences humaines, 1 Esplanade de la paix, 14000 Caen, France

Contact: louis.lebredonchel@hotmail.fr

Book written and edited by Louis Lebredonchel

Legal deposit: February 2024

Table of contents

Why I became interested in the links between food and health, and then in food education

Before delving into the heart of the matter, I thought it would be good to introduce myself and share some biographical anecdotes that led me to undertake my work and write this book.

For a little over six years, partly during my doctoral thesis, I studied the links between food and health. This writing aims to present the results of my work and the reflections that emerged from it, in the hope that my contribution can benefit its readers, on a small or large scale.

Naturally introverted and constantly immersed in my thoughts[1], I decided to pursue further studies after obtaining a master's degree in sociology research. My goal was to achieve a doctorate. Having been passionate about nutrition for a long time, especially its effects on the body and health, my initial idea was to develop a sociology of food that would consider the links between food and health, with practical implications.

Since the development of a research topic is never without connection to affinities or life experiences, a few lines about my history will shed light on the reasons behind this choice.

I won't go into detail here about my socially complex and unusual origins (due to my family's history), but let's mention that I come from a family with a relatively high cultural capital (my maternal grandfather was a teacher, intellectual, and artist from a peasant family) but low economic capital (stay-at-home mother and a father

---

[1] One can hardly go against their nature... So, I decided not to restrict my thoughts too much during the writing of this book. This means that the text you are about to read is sprinkled with numerous footnotes, sometimes lengthy, in which I elaborate on certain nuances, clarifications, and additional reflections. **Let me reassure you right away: if you find reading them tedious, it is entirely possible to go through the entire book without looking at a single one of these notes.**

who worked as a mover, passed away when I was 10, after which we experienced sudden financial instability).

An avid and passionate athlete since the age of 12, I grew up without any concrete idea of the effects my diet could have on my body. As a child and adolescent, I had significant autonomy regarding my food consumption. My mother, non-political and generally not very suspicious, also did not have a keen awareness of the potential damage of industrial and processed food on health. During my adolescence, I consumed a lot ready-made meals and highly processed foods. I didn't have major health problems, except for recurring joint issues attributed by doctors to rapid growth and overly intense physical activity.

In my early twenties, I engaged in competitive sports, often involving more than fifteen hours of training per week. I accumulated injuries and very frequent joint inflammations (tendonitis in the arms and knees, back pain, severe pubalgia making even walking difficult) for over two years, severely impairing my athletic practices. Doctors were clear: I was training too much, even excessively. Why didn't my Japanese colleagues, who trained even more than me in the same sport, have these kinds of problems?

A meeting with a chiropractor gave me the breakthrough: according to him, by changing my diet, stopping the consumption of processed and industrial foods, and consuming more raw fruits, vegetables, and quality animal products, my inflammations could be significantly reduced. I later learned that I had a chronic inflammatory disease called "ankylosing spondylitis," influenced by genetic factors[2]. According to some doctors consulted at the time, it would never be possible to engage in as much sport as before. The practice should remain occasional, at best once or twice a week, while being cautious.

---

[2] My sister and some ancestors have the same disease or similar chronic inflammatory conditions.

From that moment on (in 2014), I decided to strictly follow the advice of the chiropractor, not taking it lightly. Since then, I haven't ingested any ultra-processed food, industrial ready-made meals, soda, fast-food restaurant meals, etc. In just six months, almost all of my health problems disappeared. I gradually resumed sports and eventually increased the intensity of my training and performances.

Now having moved away from that specific sport to engage in a more general physical activity (calisthenics, fitness, running, recreational team sports, etc.), I have been practicing more than seven hours of physical activity per week for over ten years, sometimes very intense, without experiencing any problems or inflammation! I simply haven't heard about the so-called "ankylosing spondylitis" ever since.

This radical change in diet not only benefited my athletic training but, within a few months, it completely transformed my overall health and well-being. I experienced significantly increased energy, cessation of frequent headaches and sinusitis attacks, a reduction in episodes of contagious sicknesses or states of sickness during winter, a greater sense of strength, and an intensified appetite for work and knowledge. It would not be an exaggeration to say that my life changed. One might argue that all of this is merely an illusion caused by a set of psychological biases. I strongly doubt that!

As I observed these changes and gradually became aware of the crucial role of nutrition in health (while daily nourishing myself with knowledge in human nutrition and health sciences[3]), I felt a sense of injustice, even betrayal: why, since my childhood, had no one ever seriously informed me about these fundamental links? Why had I been told nothing in French schools, from nursery school to high school? Isn't it the role of the state and the education system to

---

[3] What did not happen quickly, over the course of a self-taught experience fraught with errors, understanding those errors, adjustments, and then new elements of knowledge, bis repetita. I continue, of course, to learn and feed my curiosity.

provide future adults with the necessary foundations to ensure their chances of fulfillment as citizens?

These questions prompted me to delve into food education and subsequently embark on a sociology of food and food education. What is the current curriculum teaching children about nutrition in France? How are children educated about food and its implications based on their backgrounds? According to what criteria are certain knowledge and skills transmitted to them?

This became an intriguing research topic for a sociology thesis. Gradually, as I immersed myself in daily readings of books and research articles in the sociology of food, as well as human nutrition, public health, psychology, or even history of food: the research project began to take shape.

Judged as "too ambitious" at the time, the idea of such research should find its culmination in the possibility of conducting a sociology of children's food and food education that they receive from their parents – taking into account the health implications – as well as an assessment of food education in French schools. It was also intended to propose pathways towards effective food education in schools, contributing to the prevention of chronic diseases or, more broadly, improving the long-term health of the population.

With the thesis topic decided and formulated, ideal for me and sure that I would not become bored with it over time (which is still true today), I approached potential thesis advisors within the sociology department of my university, hoping to materialize what I had already been working on independently every day.

The first professor I approached, with whom I had completed my master's thesis on a different topic, was categorical: there was no way I could undertake such research under her guidance. According to her, this did not align with sociology at all. She asserted that sociology has no business dealing with matters such as the link between individuals' food and its health implications. The project seemed to her to be "normative"; she believed it involved "moralizing people about their diet," which, in her opinion, had nothing to do with the concerns of sociology. Similar remarks have periodically recurred in the discourse of some sociologists regarding my work and approach. I find it interesting, as it raises several fundamental issues about research and its conventions, as well as interdisciplinary challenges and what I would critically call the overspecialization of sciences.

I then approached another professor qualified to supervise research, particularly concerned and active in environmental health issues. He was interested in my project and became my thesis advisor. I thank Frédérick Lemarchand for trusting me and taking my project seriously, despite its originality and the inherent risks it posed at the beginning (as well as for his guidance and advice during and after the thesis).

Later, I began to collaborate with a researcher in preventive nutrition and a Ph.D. in human nutrition. Due to a certain affinity, especially epistemologically, but also driven by the shared goal of developing strategies for effective food education in schools, he became the co-supervisor of the thesis. This interdisciplinary aspect of my project gained strength. The involvement of this researcher also encouraged me not to restrict myself too much in my pursuit of innovation.

Despite potential criticism and misunderstanding from sociologists, I was even more motivated to explore the effects of food on health and not limit my thesis work to pure sociology. I thank Anthony Fardet for his kindness, rigor, and unwavering support during the publication of our research articles.

However, I must emphasize that no one but myself is or should be held responsible for all the ideas presented in this book regarding the effects of food on health.

One of the challenges of this book is also taking a stance that a thinker, with determination and effort, can understand, assimilate, and articulate knowledge that is external to the academic discipline in which they were trained. I am not claiming that, for example, a psychologist can become a biologist through self-directed learning and then generate new knowledge in biology.

However, I do advocate the idea that a psychologist, while only capable of producing scientific knowledge in psychology based on their training, can understand and assimilate knowledge in biology (through effort) and then integrate it into an overarching logic that can enrich their work in psychology. The notion of cognitive possibilities not being limited solely to one's academic discipline is fundamental, without which the endeavor of writing this text would be absurd and irrelevant.

From this perspective, this book will not only address sociology but also health sciences, human nutrition, as well as various reflections that attempt to escape confinement in a single category or specialized discipline. It is probably important to note that I am trained and have a PhD in sociology, not nutrition or medicine. Nonetheless, this did not prevent me from delving deeply into a multitude of subjects.

I also believe that the knowledge I have acquired deserves to be shared, as it expands the understanding of the issues related to my work in sociology. My university studies in sociology and partially self-taught studies in philosophy have taught me to cultivate a synthetic mindset and an extended, global, and critical perspective on what I observe. As a professor I admired during my studies used to say, "A good intellectual is one who can connect threads between things (apparently isolated from each other) and achieve an overall vision."

This book represents an attempt to put into practice and share these developed capabilities and skills with readers. It will discuss, based on the links between nutrition and health, "why the poor are sick and how to avoid it."

Another challenge of this writing is to make complex knowledge and ideas accessible without losing nuances and precision. It is somewhat of a gamble: That one should not take the readers for more foolish than they are, while avoiding excessive simplifications and vulgarizations to cater to the commercial strategies of publishing houses (provided that clarity and simplicity in expression are maintained).

This choice led me to the path of self-publishing, without which I could not have had the freedom to produce a book that is neither purely academic (wanting to distance myself from the constraints experienced in publishing research articles) nor entirely "popularized" (simplified to the extreme to fit the commercial strategies of publishing houses).

I thank you for reading these biographical elements, and I sincerely hope that what you are about to read will be enriching and useful, in one way or another.

Notes regarding the English translation of this book

This text is a translation of my book written in French, titled "Alimentation et santé : Pourquoi les pauvres sont malades et comment l'éviter", self-published in October 2023. It revisits and summarizes most of my research works conducted in France, on children's food representations and practices, as on food education by parents and at school. Slightly shorter than the French version, one of the objectives of this book is to make my work accessible to an international audience, while attempting not to lose nuances and complexity.

I have chosen to retain numerous references from the original book, mentioning French research articles and books. I judged it preferable to keep the original references, which I am familiar with and that I consider relevant, rather than relying on new Anglo-Saxon references that might resonate better with international readers.

Additionally, as I specify in the book, my reflections and observations on food education at school primarily concern the French context, although most of my conclusions on this subject have a potentially universal scope and can extend beyond borders.

I think that the results of my research and the conclusions I have reached have significant implications, that extend beyond France. The issues highlighted, such as the fact that the poorest individuals are the most obese and suffer the most from chronic health issues, while being the ones who consume the most ultra-processed foods, are common to most Western countries and some Eastern ones. The reasons for these facts, as you are about to discover, are probably also similar across the world.

I would like to express my gratitude to foreign readers for their interest in this work, which I hope will provide them with valuable insights and a good food for thought.

Part 1: Food and health: understanding the issues

Chapter 1: The significant importance of food in our society and time

The context of epidemiological transition and chronic diseases

Since the beginning of the 20th century, an "epidemiological transition"[4] has been taking place[5]. These words refer to the shift from a high prevalence of communicable diseases and the deaths they caused to a significant increase in chronic diseases (also known as "non-communicable diseases"[6]). Currently, chronic diseases account for 7 out of the top 10 reasons for premature deaths worldwide[7] and the leading cause of early mortality in Europe. According to the WHO, by 2030, 88% of these deaths will be attributed to chronic diseases[8].

The chosen expression is even more eloquent as it signifies a transitional phase, towards which most mentalities have not yet evolved. **While communicable diseases are declining in prevalence**

---

[4] Omran A. (1971). The Epidemiological Transition: A Theory of the Epidemiology of Population Change. *The Milbank Memorial Fund Quarterly*, 49 (4), p. 509-538.

[5] While this position is unconventional, I advocate the idea that we are still in this transitional phase, precisely because the fear of viruses still prevails over that of chronic diseases in our societies.

[6] Some exceptions in terms of chronic diseases, such as AIDS, are indeed communicable in the proper sense. However, most chronic diseases, unlike communicable ones, do not develop through viruses.

[7] https://www.who.int/fr/news/item/09-12-2020-who-reveals-leading-causes-of-death-and-disability-worldwide-2000-2019

[8] World Health Organization. Global status report on non-communicable diseases 2010. April 2011.

and chronic diseases are on the rise, societal perceptions of health remain deeply rooted in the fear of communicable diseases as threats to life and human health, significantly underestimating the nature of chronic diseases.

As André Cicolella wrote, "*We remain marked by the ancestral fear of deadly infectious epidemics, such as the plague or cholera, and we still have not fully grasped the extent of the chronic disease epidemic. This same transition is happening worldwide today, but it has not yet been integrated into our perceptions and health policies*".[9]

Chronic diseases significantly differ from infectious diseases as they are not easily curable. Therefore, **it is crucial to focus our energy on prevention rather than waiting for them to develop** (as they cannot be cured by simple medical treatment, as is the case with many communicable diseases).

The causes of chronic diseases are multifactorial and complex. They are generally attributed to various factors such as smoking, **nutrition**, sedentary lifestyle and lack of physical activity, air and water quality, increased air pollutants, **or the rise of chemicals in the environment**[10].

These causes of chronic diseases partly result from interactions with the environment[11]. They are sometimes referred to as

---

[9] Cicolella A. (2013). *Toxique planète, le scandale invisible des maladies chroniques*. Paris, Éditions du Seuil.

[10] The progression of chronic diseases is also associated, beyond the mentioned causes, with an increase in life expectancy as well as an aging population. However, it is not possible to precisely assess to what extent these pathologies are linked to aging itself or to the causes mentioned above, especially since life expectancy has increased simultaneously with the degradation of our interactions with the environment. Chronic diseases can also depend on genetic factors, which interact with the mentioned causes or are sometimes even a part of their consequences (I will come back to this).

[11] "Environment" is understood here in both the sense of «everything that is not genetic or innate» and to refer to the earth, air, soils, water, agriculture, livestock,

"environmental pathologies," stemming from a prolonged deterioration of our interactions with the environment over the past century. Some speak of the emergence of "environmental health" as a departure from an old "hygienist" conception of health. However, it is still considered a specific branch rather than the foundation of overall health.

The most common chronic diseases include obesity, type 2 diabetes, cardiovascular diseases, cancers, respiratory diseases, neurological diseases, autoimmune diseases, chronic joint and bone problems, as well as reproductive disorders.

Just as their causes are multiple and interconnected, chronic diseases can influence and trigger one another. For example, obesity is often correlated with the development of type 2 diabetes, cardiovascular pathologies, certain cancers, or chronic joint problems.

Due to their chronic nature, **these diseases result in a significant increase in the time spent in poor health** (or years of healthy life lost[12]) and a total decline in the quality of life for patients (on psychological, professional, emotional, socioeconomic, etc., levels).

Moreover, **they represent a considerable cost on a national and international scale**; estimates from 2011 predicted that expenses related to chronic diseases would be around 2,350 billion per year for the next two decades[13].

The books and movies I was exposed to during my childhood promised a future of technological progress, giving way to dreams,

---

as well as everything that contributes to feeding us and to which we are exposed daily.

[12] Murray C.J. (2012). Global Burden of Disease 2010: a multi-investigator collaboration for global comparative descriptive epidemiology. *The Lancet*, vol. 380/9859, p. 2055-2058. https://doi.org/10.1016/S0140-6736(12)62134-5

[13] World Economic Forum, Havard School of Public Health. (2011). The Global Economic Burden of Non-communicable Diseases.

flying cars, space travel, and life in space. The present is leading us towards a nightmarish world of chronic illnesses and poverty, facets of the same reality that is becoming increasingly fatal.

Parallel to the evolution of chronic diseases, what are known as "social inequalities in health" are growing. **The most vulnerable populations are the most affected by most of these pathologies** (particularly in the West). This is, for example, the case with obesity[14]. In France, obese individuals are overrepresented among socially and economically disadvantaged children, adolescents, and adults.

As you may have understood, chronic diseases are a real disaster for society. According to the UN, they represent "*one of the main challenges for development in the 21st century.*"[15] This implies a need to change our entire healthcare system, which is still heavily focused on treatment, to allocate more resources to prevention.

This idea has been explicitly stated by the leaders of UN member countries: "*We, Heads of State and Government... recognize the primary role of governments and the responsibility they bear in addressing the challenge of non-communicable diseases and the urgent need for all sectors of society to act and engage in generating effective responses for prevention and control of these diseases.*"[16]

I imagine I am not the only one wondering where these actions by "all sectors of society" for preventing these diseases have actually gone. It must be said that the world has somewhat changed since 2011, and many political, economic, and budgetary decisions,

---

[14] Devaux M., Sassi F. (2013). Social inequalities in obesity and overweight in 11 OECD countries. *European Journal of Public Health*, Volume 23, Issue 3, June 2013, Pages 464–469, https://doi.org/10.1093/eurpub/ckr058; Robertson A., Lobstein T., Knai C. (2007), Obesity and socio-economic groups in Europe: evidence review and implications for action. Brussels: European Commission.

[15] Article 1 of the United Nations General Assembly declaration of September 2011, signed by leaders of 184 countries in New York.

[16] *Ibid*.

especially in the management of Covid-19, have not brought us closer to such total commitment to the prevention of chronic diseases[17]. Although this observation is made for France, I believe it is also applicable to most Western countries.

Nevertheless, as I write these lines, the measures taken do not yet seem to be moving towards sufficient attention from the government and all sectors of society for the prevention of chronic diseases. Hoping for changes to come soon, I am trying to contribute to advancing things by drawing attention to food.

Food as an empowerment: a daily interaction with the environment, partially chosen but limited by constraints

While all interactions with the environment are crucial for health, potentially playing a role in preventing chronic diseases or, conversely, influencing their development, **I have chosen to focus on food**.

Indeed, food constitutes one of our primary relationships with the environment. Assuming we consume three meals per day and live an average of 80 years (in France), we consume approximately 80,000 meals in a lifetime. It is essential to note that each food item eaten during these meals significantly influences the production of hormones, our immune system, energy levels, and our body's ability to combat assaults and preserve cell health[18].

In general, **food can either contribute to preventing chronic diseases and maintaining good health or, conversely, foster the development of chronic diseases and contribute to weakening our health**. Before delving into which foods contribute to each direction,

---

[17] This is not a critique of the management of Covid-19 (which I will refrain from making), but a simple observation.

[18] These few mentioned mechanisms influenced by food consumption are all interconnected with regard to health.

let's focus on the advantages and challenges presented by food in this context.

Food appears as the most controllable interaction with the environment by humans on an individual scale. Indeed, if one wants to optimize the air or water quality of a territory, the only possibilities for action involve social actions or political measures (which are only feasible over time, requiring significant energy and time investments, typically in organized groups[19]). In contrast, an individual's diet depends, at least in theory and principle, only on themselves and their daily choices. **In this sense, food constitutes an empowerment, first on oneself and then on the environment.**

"In theory and principle" because it is evident that reality is more complex, and individuals' dietary choices are not solely a matter of will, independent of their living conditions. I will distinguish two main categories of limits to the idea of free food consumption[20]: economic and budgetary constraints and sociocultural factors.

It would indeed be incongruous to describe food solely as an empowerment without considering the constraints, especially economic and budgetary ones, that limit it. Ultra-processed foods, which promote the development of chronic diseases and are detrimental to health, can sometimes cost up to 50% less than raw

---

[19] However, if these groups do not face pressure from lobbies, which generally diminish the ability of individuals to act, even once formed into groups

[20] Production, as an alternative to consumption, is still much more limited today (due to budgetary, heritage, temporal, spatial constraints, and many others).

or minimally processed foods[21], making them generally more accessible for modest budgets[22].

Concerning ultra-processed foods, it has been observed that in most rich and developed Western countries, such as France[23], the most precarious populations consume them the most[24].

Raw and unprocessed foods, such as fruits, vegetables and quality animal products that, unlike ultra-processed foods, help combat chronic diseases and protect our health in general and within a balanced diet[25], tend to be more expensive and are consumed less

---

[21] Gupta S., Hawk T., Aggarwal A., Drewnowski A. (2019). Characterizing ultra-processed foods by energy density, nutrient density, and cost. *Frontiers in Nutrition*, 6, 70, https://doi.org/10.3389/fnut.2019.00070; Vandevijvere S., Pedroni C., De Ridder K., Castetbon K. (2020). The cost of diets according to their caloric share of ultraprocessed and minimally processed foods in Belgium. *Nutrients*, 12, 9, 2787, https://doi.org/10.3390/nu12092787

[22] This is actually only true for developed Western countries, but it's rather the opposite in some so-called developing countries, such as Brazil or Mexico, where ultra-processed foods are more expensive than local raw and minimally processed foods. See: Simões B., Barreto, S.M., Molina M., Luft V.C., Duncan B.B., Schmidt M.I., Benseñor I., Cardoso L.O., Levy R.B., Giatti L. (2018). Consumption of ultra-processed foods and socioeconomic position: a cross-sectional analysis of the Brazilian Longitudinal Study of Adult Health (ELSA-Brasil). *Cadernos de saude publica*, 34(3), e00019717. https://doi.org/10.1590/0102-311X00019717; Marrón-Ponce J., Sánchez-Pimienta T., Louzada M.L.C., Batis C. (2018). Energy contribution of NOVA food groups and sociodemographic determinants of ultra-processed food consumption in the Mexican population. *Public health nutrition*, 21(1), 87–93. https://doi.org/10.1017/S1368980017002129

[23] Julia C., Martinez L., Allès B., Touvier M., Hercberg S., Méjean C., Kesse-Guyot E. (2018). Contribution of ultra-processed foods in the diet of adults from the French NutriNet-Santé study. *Public Health Nutrition*, 21(1), 27–37. https://doi.org/10.1017/S1368980017001367

[24] The situation is different in most developing countries, where ultra-processed foods are often seen as symbols of openness to the world and progress. In several South American or Asian countries, ultra-processed foods are more consumed by the wealthier and more educated individuals.

[25] One should also avoid falling into an oversimplified view that suggests the more fruits, vegetables, or plant-based foods one consumes, the better it is for health. For instance, it is known that consuming excessive amounts of fruits can eventually prove detrimental, especially due to significant carbohydrate intake (fructose and

by lower-income families and more by economically prosperous households.

Additionally, foods from organic farming and animal husbandry, whose production is not supposed to be linked to the use of pesticides, are generally[26] healthier than products from so-called "conventional" production, which does not shy away from the use of multiple pathogenic chemicals.

I won't need to cite research articles here to remind you that organic-labeled products always cost more for consumers, limiting lower-income households in their ability to buy them regularly. (Although a French study found that consumers of organic products are not systematically wealthier than those who do not buy them and that, with equivalent incomes, frequent consumers have higher levels of education and physical activity[27].)

Some sociological research has also claimed that the ability of low-budget households to eat healthily is constrained by both "budgetary limitations" and restrictions related to the time and energy required for the preparation of healthy meals[28] (industrial

---

sucrose). (See: Alami F., Alizadeh M., Shateri K. (2022). The effect of a fruit-rich diet on liver biomarkers, insulin resistance, and lipid profile in patients with non-alcoholic fatty liver disease: a randomized clinical trial. *Scandinavian journal of gastroenterology*, 57(10), 1238–1249. https://doi.org/10.1080/00365521.2022.2071109). Hence the importance of a balanced and varied diet: I will come back to this in a section dedicated to what I consider to be a healthy diet.

[26] It is necessary to qualify this statement by distinguishing theoretical and labeled "organic," which is precisely a label with all the biases that it implies, such as the possibility of cultivating organic plants by the side of a highway. And truly practical organic productions, not necessarily always certified.

[27] Kesse-Guyota E., Péneaua S., Méjeana C., Szabo de Edelenyia F., Galana P., Hercberg S., Laironc D. (2013). Profil des consommateurs de produits bio en France : premières données de l'Étude Nutrinet-Santé. *Innovations Agronomiques*, Volume 32.

[28] Ditlevsen K., Halkier B., Holm L. (2022). Pathways of less healthy diets. An investigation of the everyday food practices of men and women in low income

and ultra-processed dishes often being ready-made and reheatable, while raw foods demand more time and energy investment for preparation).

Are we at an impasse here? Are the poorest, who are most affected by most chronic diseases and obesity, condemned or "determined" to consume unhealthy foods due to their budgetary restrictions[29]? Although I acknowledge the possibility of such reasoning, I will clarify that it is not my position.

Several factors allow us to move away from a deterministic and homo-economicus perception of food consumption[30]. This includes culture, education, social norms, and a critical and contextual perspective on dietary behaviors. In other words, **a consistent sociological approach allows us to break free from the view that dietary choices are entirely determined by economic constraints.**

Eating is also and above all a matter of culture and education

According to a report from ANSES[31] published in 2012 on the diet of French children and adolescents, **the parents' level of education would influence the quality of the diet (of children and adolescents) more than their income.** Could education, and more broadly, culture, have a greater impact on diet than economic constraints? First and foremost, let's be clear that we cannot drastically oppose culture (and all that this word implies in terms of representations, norms, habits, etc.) and income, as both are

---

households. *Critical* *Public* *Health,* https://doi.org/10.1080/09581596.2022.2101917

[29] This would more or less amount to thinking, "the poor have no choice but to eat poorly, so we might as well let them do it... "

[30] According to which man would be a purely rational being whose actions are primarily driven by calculations, especially economic ones.

[31] Anses. (2012). Disparités socio-économiques et apports alimentaires et nutritionnels des enfants et adolescents. Rapport d'étude, Paris, Anses.

intrinsically linked and significantly intertwined, especially in the concept of "social classes."

I think that, although limited by budget constraints, dietary behaviors are also strongly influenced by culture and are therefore likely to be shaped or evolved through education.

In this regard, Claude Fischler's sociology teaches us that individuals' dietary choices should not be understood as oriented solely toward what is biologically edible but also (and perhaps more importantly[32]) toward what is "culturally edible"[33]. The act of eating can thus be considered an activity that is partly "socially constructed," as it varies across space and time. We do not eat in the same way in France today as we did 1000 years ago[34], nor do people in Europe and East Asia eat the same way today. Moreover, individuals exist only as members of social groups, with representations, tastes, and cultures unique to them.

Thus, individuals' food consumption choices cannot be reduced to purely rational motivations, optimizing their health or based on their budget. According to Claude Fischler, *"In every culture, there are rules of great complexity that govern food consumption and the eater's behavior based on established classifications. These culinary rules are internalized by individuals in a largely unconscious way."*[35]

---

[32] This idea seems all the more true as it is not irrelevant to question the real edibility of certain modern artificial products, yet very "culturally edible" (having no difficulty in reaching their consumers, notably due to considerable influences of marketing).

[33] Fischler C. (1990). *L'Homnivore : Le goût, la cuisine et le corps*. Paris, Odile Jacob.

[34] Beyond purely cultural differences that have led to changes in representations and eating behaviors, it is important to understand that availabilities and accessibility in terms of resources, techniques, production technology, preservation, etc., have also played significant roles. This reflection invites us to reconsider the connections between the construction of social representations and culture, and the available resources in a given society.

[35] [35] *Ibid.*

We particularly note here the theoretical significance of the unconscious manner in which individuals internalize "culinary rules," depending on their culture and education.

We also know that food marketing has a massive influence on consumption choices[36], proving in a way that eating is a malleable practice.

However, in our health and social context, should it not be more beneficial to children's health (and the population's health) through education rather than to the enrichment of multinational corporations through marketing?

The work of Nicolas Herpin and Daniel Verger shows that **since 1960, the share of the French budget spent on food has gradually decreased, while the share devoted to healthcare and medicines has continuously increased** (despite the fact that in France, social security covers a significant portion of these expenses). Food products, which represented 22.4% of the effective consumption of the French in 1960, corresponded to 10.6% in 2006. As for expenses related to health, care, and medicines, "*the budgetary coefficient of the effective household consumption, which was 5.2% in 1960, 7.4% in 1970, and 9.0% in 1980, rose to 11.4% in 2000, reaching 11.9% in 2006.*"[37]

While considering that these changes correspond to averages calculated on the consumption of all French people, these data at least allow us to observe a significant reduction in the percentage of the budget dedicated to food, coexisting with an increase in that

---

[36] It is largely through marketing that ultra-processed breakfast cereals, specifically marketed for children, have established themselves as norms, popularized with the creation of charismatic heroes designed to appeal to them. Additionally, of course, they reassure parents by promoting health virtues that they do not possess.

[37] Herpin N., Verger D. (2008). *Consommation et modes de vie en France, Une approche économique et sociologique sur un demi-siècle.* Paris, La découverte.

dedicated to healthcare and medicines. According to me, this change has two significant theoretical issues.

Firstly, **this may indicate that, despite the increase in the prevalence of chronic diseases (which, let's remember, requires more resources for prevention than for treatment[38]), the consumption habits of the French have evolved towards less attention to food (and probably prevention), leaning more towards curative measures.**

Secondly, this decrease in the percentage of the budget dedicated to food in France could also mean that the French, in general, could afford to dedicate more to their diet than they currently do (perhaps also if they had less need to spend this money on the consumption of medicines and healthcare). One might argue here, shocked by my statements, that it is already very difficult for certain less affluent segments of the population to feed themselves. Having investigated among children from very poor families and encountered a few cases, albeit exceptional, who were not eating enough and were probably malnourished, I can only support this counter-argument.

Still, **it is highly probable that if the French, or individuals in general, did not have to spend so much money on medicines and healthcare (though limited in the face of chronic diseases[39]), they could afford to invest more in a healthy daily diet.**

It is also possible that this decrease in the percentage of the budget devoted to food in France may be due to other multiple factors: such as a constant increase in the consumption of household appliances and technology products since the post-World War II period; a relative trust in the "safety" of industrial foods (food safety is still today to be understood according to a hygienist and bacteriological paradigm of health); or the fact, mentioned earlier, that collective

---

[38] Not that care is not important, but because it is much easier and more effective to prevent them than to cure them.

[39] Medications often act on the symptoms of the pathology, and less on its origins.

consciousness tends to remain anchored in the fear of communicable diseases, generally overlooking chronic diseases and their parameters.

To be clear, this is by no means an attempt to over-responsibilize individuals or, even less, to accuse the French of having too low an interest or share of their budget dedicated to food. However, it seems important to remain nuanced[40] when studying what motivates individuals' food consumption choices, without falling into systematic victimization ("the poor cannot do otherwise than eat ultra-processed foods"), suggesting that real changes are not possible.

The rich tend to eat healthier than the poor: is it truly a problem?

The qualitative sociology investigation I conducted, along with several studies in humanities and social sciences, has revealed the following:

1) **Individuals from disadvantaged backgrounds consume more ultra-processed foods and fewer whole and non-processed foods (including fruits, vegetables, and animal products) than individuals from affluent social positions.**

2) **Individuals from affluent backgrounds place particular importance on avoiding industrial food products made from ingredients they distrust, opting instead for authentic, homemade, and often organic foods.**

Is this genuinely a problem? It may be thought otherwise. This perspective is commonly encountered, especially in anonymous discussions with sociologists, notably during peer-reviewed

---

[40] By avoiding the traps and limitations of determinism ("it's because of society and not individuals") or individualism ("individuals are entirely responsible for their choices"), which become empty and without nuances when they confine themselves to their respective polarities.

26

research article publications. This standpoint primarily emphasizes that each culture has legitimate characteristics. While it's interesting to study and understand them in sociology, considering the representations or behaviors specific to a social group as "problematic" is out of the question.

This position may seem reasonable and coherent, aligning with the role of a sociology researcher: to study social reality as it is, without passing value judgments[41]. Furthermore, if there is a perceived problem in the described facts, how could it be resolved? Any attempt to bring about change, aiming for shifts in the dietary habits of the most vulnerable populations, might be seen as illegitimate imposition of practices not their own. **"Each to their culture, habits, practices, and customs" is a stance often found in sociological discourses.**

However, I, holding a PhD in sociology, don't believe that only the "social" dimension of this reality should be considered. Let's now integrate other facts, external to what is purely "social" but shouldn't be ignored:

3) **Ultra-processed foods are significantly associated with the development of multiple chronic diseases[42], including obesity.**

4) **A diet based on consuming unprocessed foods (including quality animal products, fruit and vegetable[43]), as part of a balanced diet,**

---

[41] From a positivist perspective: sociology is a science, and the scientist must be as neutral as possible towards their object of study, while being well aware of the cognitive limits to achieving this neutrality.

[42] Pagliai G., Dinu M., Madarena M.P., Bonaccio M., Iacoviello L., Sofi F. (2020). Consumption of ultra-processed foods and health status: a systematic review and meta-analysis. *British Journal of Nutrition*, 125, 308-318, https://doi.org/10.1017/S0007114520002688 ; Chen X., Zhang Z., Yang H., Qiu P., Wang H., Wang F., Zhao Q., Fang J., Nie J. (2020). Consumption of ultra-processed foods and health outcomes: a systematic review of epidemiological studies. *Nutrition journal*, 19(1), 86, https://doi.org/10.1186/s12937-020-00604-1

[43] Volpe S.L. (2019). Fruit and Vegetable Intake and Prevention of Chronic Disease. *ACSM's Health & Fitness Journal*, 5/6 2019, Volume 23, Issue 3, p 30-31. https://doi.org/10.1249/FIT.0000000000000474 ; Hung H.C., Joshipura K.J., Jiang

contributes to preventing these same chronic diseases while promoting overall health.

Returning to new social information:

5) **The most vulnerable populations are the most affected by obesity and most chronic diseases.**

6) **Social health inequalities have generally increased**[44] **over the last forty years**[45].

The six mentioned facts seem eloquent and serious enough to be considered a genuine problem that warrants resolution. Summarizing this in a single sentence: **the poorest individuals have food habitus**[46] **that promote the development of chronic diseases (including obesity) and are the most obese and unwell. Moreover, nothing concrete is being done, or institutionally organized and planned, to effectively combat this phenomenon.**

R., Hu F.B., Hunter D., Smith-Warner S.A., Colditz G.A., Rosner B., Spiegelman D., Willett W.C. (2004). Fruit and vegetable intake and risk of major chronic disease. *Journal of the National Cancer Institute*, 96(21), 1577–1584. https://doi.org/10.1093/jnci/djh296

[44] Of course, it is not a matter of interpreting this phenomenon in a reductionist way, claiming that this evolution is solely due to the increase in the prevalence of chronic diseases.

[45] Alvarenga A., Bana e Costa C.A., Borrell C. et al. (2019. Scenarios for population health inequalities in 2030 in Europe: the EURO-HEALTHY project experience. *International Journal for Equity in Health*, 18, 100. https://doi.org/10.1186/s12939-019-1000-8

[46] In sociology, drawing on concepts from Pierre Bourdieu and Norbert Elias, habitus is defined as a "lasting way of behaving, speaking, walking, [...] feeling, and thinking," internalized as a "second nature" and playing a significant role in constructing "both individual and collective identity of members within a human group, whether it be a family, a company, a political party, or a nation."

Summarizing the more theoretical implications expressed so far: **food represents a daily interaction with the environment that can either contribute to preventing chronic diseases or, conversely, promote their development. Eating represents a power to act, as consumption choices are theoretically free. However, it is restricted by budgetary constraints and remains complex due to strong influences from social and cultural factors. In broad terms, it is known that the most vulnerable have a diet that promotes the development of multiple chronic diseases, and they are the sickest.**

The problem of budgetary constraints related to eating cannot be solved without very significant social, political, economic, or even systemic changes that would profoundly disrupt society.

However, **couldn't the influence of cultural factors on diet represent a potential opportunity to contribute to the fight against chronic diseases and social inequalities in health?**

In other words, **could implementing food education in schools contribute to positively influencing (for health) dietary representations and practices through learning and culture?** (In contrast to advertising food marketing targeting children, almost always to sell ultra-processed foods[47], which succeeds in influencing them deleteriously for their health.)

What about food education in french schools?

At the time I am writing these lines, there is still no systematic food education in French public schools and in the national education system, which would be implemented based on a program common to institutions, differentiated according to the stages of the academic journey, and monitored by academic inspectors. This passage will not consist of a comprehensive overview or a report on all legislative and institutional advances, associative or local actions in France regarding food education in schools, but rather reflections inherent to the role that public schools could play, along with some observations.

Given the challenges outlined, the idea of food education in schools seems absolutely logical, and its implementation is crucial. Public schools, responsible for the transmission of knowledge and common rules to future citizens, children, and adolescents, both in their interest and the general interest of society, could indeed

---

[47] Mallarino C., Gómez L.F., González-Zapata L., Cadena Y., Parra D.C. (2013). Advertising of ultra-processed foods and beverages: children as a vulnerable population. *Revista De Saude Publica*, 47 (5): 1006–1010. https://doi.org/10.1590/s0034-8910.2013047004319 ; Martines R.M., Machado P.P, Neri D.A., Levy R.B., Rauber F. (2019). Association between watching TV whilst eating and children's consumption of ultraprocessed foods in United Kingdom. *Maternal & Child Nutrition*, 15 (4). e12819. https://doi.org/10.1111/mcn.12819

enable all children to acquire a set of knowledge regarding the links between food and health.

Contrasting theories about the challenges of food education in schools

A "deterministic" sociological perspective might suggest that such a measure would be unnecessary, assuming that food preferences are solely transmitted from parents to children, following class habits. According to the French sociologist Pierre Bourdieu, dietary preferences transmitted by the family represent "*the strongest and most unalterable mark of primitive learning, those that survive the longest distance or the collapse of the native world and sustain its nostalgia most enduringly.*"[48] In conjunction with such a deterministic view, the idea of food education in schools is often assimilated to biopower[49] (i.e., a desire for control of bodies by an institution, with health as a pretext). It can also be perceived as the imposition of a dominant discourse dictating "good practices" to populations whose culture does not align with them.

Even when one does not share this position, these are important considerations to take into account, **especially because nutrition seems not to be learned in the same way as mathematics or geometry**. Eating is an act strongly linked to the eater's intimacy: psychologically, physically, and symbolically, due to the penetration into the body, ingestion, and digestion of food; as well as to their identity, due to its social and cultural dimensions.

These parameters imply approaching food education in schools differently than teaching other knowledges that does not affect

---

[48] Bourdieu P. (1979). *La Distinction : critique sociale du jugement*. Paris, Les Éditions de minuit.

[49] Leahy D., Wright J. (2016). Governing food choices: A critical analysis of school food pedagogies and young people's responses in contemporary times. *Cambridge Journal of Education,* 46(2), 233-246. http://doi.org/10.1080/0305764X.2015.1118440

students' intimacy and identity in the same way, or else it could be perceived as mere health injunctions (which tends not to work, especially among lower classes. I will come back to this point and elaborate on it later).

These few limits and theoretical considerations regarding food education in schools, however, do not question all the benefits it could bring, both to students and society as a whole. Beyond the deterministic and critical perspectives introduced above, **other theoretical reflections seem to support the idea that food education in schools could positively influence the representations and practices of future citizens through instruction, culture, and sociability**.

According to sociologist Claude Fischler, it is not only the transmission of parents' tastes to children that allows them to internalize they own norms and tastes, but also the daily and repeated experience of children with their food[50]. **The school, as a place of daily learning and socialization outside the family sphere, thus represents an opportunity to provide children with an alternative nutritional experience to that lived with their family**. Based on several studies by Leann L. Birch, an American psychologist, on what influences children's diet, Claude Fischler states that:

"Studies on correlations between parental and child food preferences show that this correlation is weak and not significantly different from what can be found between the food preferences of children and parents of other children in the same school (Birch, 1988). In other words, the existing relationship should be attributed to other factors (socio-cultural or others) rather than the direct influence of parents on children. [...] The most important factor in

---

[50] Fischler C. (1990). *L'Homnivore : Le goût, la cuisine et le corps. op.cit.*

expanding and socializing a child's food preferences is the direct influence of peers."[51]

These considerations led me to think that, although some critiques of food education in schools commonly found among researchers must be taken into account, the school still represents a major opportunity to bring about changes in the tastes and food practices of children (and thus future adults).

Food education in schools in France, a still-emerging and shaky project

Although my study focused on France that fact that and I did not investigate practices within each international country, it appears that many other places are in a similar or comparable situation to France (such as the USA, where children receive less than 8 hours of nutrition education per year). **I have decided to keep this passage in the English version of my book, notwithstanding that my considerations about what is practiced (or not) in France may not be of interest to foreign readers. If that is the case, I invite you to proceed to the next section of the book.**

While the idea of food education in schools to improve public health, taking into account the social and cultural dimensions of nutrition, now seems self-evident, reality still faces a set of difficulties to achieve this. In fact, the latter is already included in the French education code[52], and has been for some years now. However, it remains an embryonic project, as:

---

[51] *Ibid.*

[52] For example, according to Article L312-17-3 (dated February 13, 2016), which stipulates that "*information and education on nutrition and the fight against food waste, consistent with the guidelines of the national program on nutrition and health mentioned in Article L. 3231-1 of the Public Health Code and the national program for food mentioned in Article L. 1 of the Rural Code and Maritime Fishing, are provided in educational institutions, as part of the curriculum or the territorial educational project mentioned in Article L. 551-1 of this code [...].*"

Its objectives are multiple, blending and confusing between the fight against food waste, the fight against overweight and obesity, "environmental"[53] issues and challenges, or the transmission of knowledge about agriculture and livestock. In other words, it does not seem to have been clearly defined and specified to what extent it should aim for education in the service of health or education in a very broad framework, intended to raise awareness of a set of other subjects. Although those related to health and the environment are not mutually exclusive[54], it remains important to distinguish them, as well as to avoid straying too far from health issues.

The lack of precision in the education code or official texts from the Ministry of Education (or other state institutions) regarding the objectives of food education is also due to the absence of an associated program. In France, the school program is linked to the mandatory nature of teaching, which must be controlled by academic inspectors. **Currently, food education in schools resembles what is commonly referred to as "education about."** These, like "environmental education," "education for sustainable development," "education for gender equality," or "education against racism and antisemitism," are supposed to be provided by schools according to laws and articles of the education code, but their implementation is not controlled by inspectors. Teachers find themselves faced with a complex set of "educations about" to address. However, since they are not or very little trained in these matters and already have to provide numerous mandatory teachings, they are generally unmotivated, often considering that these subjects remain external to their functions[55].

---

[53] It must be acknowledged that this term remains often vague even today, as it can be used to refer to both pollution and environmental health, as well as the forecasts for temperature increase established by the IPCC.

[54] Human health always depends on the state of its environment.

[55] Gauthier R.F. (2014). *Ce que l'école devrait enseigner, pour une révolution de la politique scolaire en France*. Paris, Dunos.

As a result, food education in schools today in France, despite having a place in the education code, is implemented randomly, according to teachers' willingness, motivation, or sensitivity to this subject, without them having received training in this field.

It is obviously challenging to envision food education in schools without teachers being trained themselves, or at least aware, of the challenges of food concerning health (which does not yet seem self-evident). A major step forward on this front would therefore involve:

- Teachers, from elementary school to secondary school, receiving training in food education;

- This training being carefully developed, based in particular on research in social sciences and education sciences, as well as in human nutrition and health sciences;

- Food education being integrated into school programs, which implies that it is taken over by academic inspectors of national education, thus moving away from its current optional nature as "education about."

However, this latter possibility faces the difficulty that it would still be necessary for food to be considered by elected officials as more important than societal issues that have been voted on and included in the education code as different types of "education about." The problem is that eating always tends to be perceived precisely as a "societal problem" rather than as a fundamental activity essential to the survival of our species (which it actually is).

I may be reproached for delivering an activist discourse here, emphasizing a subject to which I am particularly sensitive and concerned. Additionally, any associative movement, individual, or political figure could entirely develop the same type of reasoning for another subject currently included in the framework of "education about," claiming, through a well-developed (or not) argument, that this topic is absolutely crucial and should not be approached randomly and optionally in schools. Are we in an impasse regarding the possibility of systematic food education being consistently implemented in schools in France and anchored in school programs? Only time will tell.

Meanwhile, I hope that reading this book and discovering my work will help its readers understand the importance of these issues.

Objectives of the sociology survey

It is the combination of these theoretical elements that led me to conduct a sociology survey as part of my doctoral thesis.

The idea came to me to study the representations and eating behaviors of children, as well as the question of food education by parents and in elementary schools. Indeed, to advance knowledge in the field of food education, it seemed essential to first focus on the diet of children and the food education transmitted by their parents.

The envisaged survey was designed to help me achieve the following objectives:

- **Propose a sociology of food of French children (and, through them, access a more general analysis of food within families).**

- **Conduct a study on food education by parents and in the schools where I would conduct the survey.**

- **Based on the two previous objectives: Reflect on strategies for food education in schools contributing to combating chronic diseases and social inequalities in health, based on the survey results (grounded in the reality of the field).**

In doing so, I also developed what I would call a "sociology of food, conscious about links between food and health."

This approach has earned me numerous critiques[56], suggesting that what I am doing is not truly sociology, or that as a sociologist, I should not involve myself in anything other than a purely "social" dimension. Confident in my initiative and its contribution to research, I assert that it has the advantage of addressing social realities concerning food without separating them from their "physical" and health-related implications.

Before presenting the results of this survey and the outcomes of this work, I think it is important to outline what, in my opinion, corresponds and does not correspond to what constitutes a diet good for health. In other words, I aim to explain what I mean by this "consciousness of the links between food and health."

---

[56] Both by research article reviewers, with whom I had to struggle to have them published in conventional sociology journals, and up to my thesis defense by certain members of the jury.

Chapter 2: What constitutes a healthy diet and what doesn't?

This section does not aim to provide an exhaustive analysis of what is and isn't a healthy diet, but rather a synthesis attempting to present the aspects and issues that seem most essential to me. This approach is not without risk, as it would have been less subject to criticism and more comfortable to stick to the domain that is (only?) supposed to concern me according to my academic specialization: sociology. After all, what business do I have meddling in this? I don't hold any state diplomas in human nutrition or dietetics. It is crucial to emphasize that I do not claim to possess the same expertise as a nutritionist or dietitian. So, why take the time to delve into what, in my opinion, constitutes a healthy diet?

The reason is that I have been interested, passionate, and dedicated to studying this subject for over 10 years[57]. As you may understand, because I don't believe that one should deprive oneself or forbid oneself from delving deeply into things outside their specific discipline, even if it involves a detailed examination. In fact, **the added value that this consciousness of the links between food and health brings to sociological research on food appears so substantial to me that it would be regrettable not to address this aspect.**

I could have simply referred to some so-called "consensual" scientific references without actively participating in the discussion. However, I consider it fundamental, at least to attempt to deepen our understanding of the subject: which requires assimilating a significant amount of information, articulating it, and developing a critical perspective. Although I haven't studied human nutrition within a university curriculum, I have acquired certain skills in synthesis and critical thinking. **This allows me, among other things,**

---

[57] In theory and in practice, 365 days a year.

to connect various complex pieces of information in a coherent overall logic, and that's precisely the exercise we will engage in here.

My study of the links between food and health has led me to develop a conception of what constitutes and doesn't constitute a healthy diet along three main axes.

First Axis: Eating real with a whole foods based diet, or the importance of the food matrix and the consequences of its degradation

What is the food matrix?

It is not easy to present and attempt to explain, in a brief synthesis, the major importance of what the food matrix represents in terms of health issues. However, the essence of what needs to be known could be conveyed in the following sentence: "**We consume food matrices, not just nutrients**[58]". This statement could also be formulated as follows: "**For our health, we should consume non-degraded matrices, not just nutrients potentially separated from their matrix.**"

The food matrix is the food in its entirety, as a living organism[59] with its own existence and reality that cannot be reduced to the sum of the nutrients it contains.

---

[58] Fardet A. (2018). Choisir des aliments non transformés. *L'écologiste*, n°53, vol 19 n°3.

[59] Or a freshly deceased organism, in the case of animal products such as meat and fish.

Let's take the example of two fruits we are all familiar with, an apple and a banana. We can study what makes up both fruits in terms of "nutritional values"[60] and find results such as:

An apple is partly composed of approximately[61] 12g of carbohydrates, 110g of potassium, between 1.5g and 2.5g of fiber, and 85g of water.

A banana is partly composed of approximately 19g of carbohydrates, 320g of potassium, 3g of fiber, and 75g of water.

We can delve further into the breakdown of the nutritional components of the two fruits, noting that the carbohydrates in a banana and an apple (mainly consisting of sucrose, glucose, fructose, and starch), although not equal in quantity, have many similarities. Both fruits also share, for example, the commonality of being rich in pectin. **So, in terms of nutritional values and compositions, the apple and banana have many similarities, right?**

However, anyone who has eaten at least one banana and one apple in their life will have noticed that the two fruits are quite different: they do not taste the same, do not have the same smell, and have different textures. **This is because they are two different foods and two different living organisms!** Moreover, they are fruits from distinct organisms that do not evolve in the same climates, do not resemble each other, and do not have the same energy needs, etc.

At this point, you might feel like you're being taken for fools; these are common sense and highly logical observations. Nevertheless,

---

[60] In nutrition, it is customary to speak of the «nutritional value» of a food to refer to its quantities of nutrient components. However, this can be questioned, as the term «value» should not be misleading, often causing confusion between the quantitative value of the nutrients that make up the food and a distorted idea of the qualitative value of the food. The health effects of a food cannot be reduced to its levels of nutritional components: that is the whole challenge of what I am trying to explain there.

[61] These are approximate numbers that will vary depending on the ripeness of an apple or banana, as well as their varieties.

they are of fundamental importance because they illustrate that **food cannot be reduced to the nutrients it contains. It is a complete organism with its origins and its own existence, not just an aggregation of nutritional components. The term "food matrix" is used to define food as a whole, as an organism, not reducible to the sum of its nutrients.**

The matrix effect

The expression "matrix effect" is used to describe the fact that, **"With a strictly identical composition of nutrients but different matrices, two foods will not have the same impact on the body and, therefore, in the long term, on health."**[62]

Indeed, nutrients will not behave in the same way and will not interact in the same manner with our bodies depending on their food matrix. Similarly, the way they are ingested, either as part of their original matrix (in their original food) or isolated from it, also plays a role[63].

Let's take an apple as an example again. It has been observed that when an apple is eaten as it is, according to its original matrix, it somehow has a "better" interaction with our bodies than when it has been turned into applesauce or juice[64]. What do I mean by better interaction? In fact, reducing the apple to applesauce or juice, by deconstructing its matrix, alters and decreases its natural qualitative and quantitative fiber content, affecting glucose

---

[62] Fardet A. (2017). L'effet matrice des aliments, un nouveau concept. *Pratiques en nutrition*, n°52, http://doi.org/10.1016/j.pranut.2017.09.009

[63] Aguilera J.M. (2018). The food matrix: implications in processing, nutrition and health. *Critical Reviews in Food Science and Nutrition*, 59(22), 3612–3629. https://doi.org/10.1080/10408398.2018.1502743

[64] Haber G.B., Heaton K.W., Murphy D., Burroughs L.F. (1977). Depletion and disruption of dietary fibre. Effects on satiety, plasma-glucose, and serum-insulin. *Lancet* (London, England), 2(8040), 679–682. https://doi.org/10.1016/s0140-6736(77)90494-9

homeostasis, insulin release, and the produced satiety, as they would normally occur after ingesting a whole apple. All of this has few negative effects on blood sugar levels, which are higher after consuming applesauce or juice than after eating a whole apple[65]. **This generally means that by altering or degrading the matrix of a food, we modify the interaction it is supposed to have with the body** (from an evolutionary perspective).

This is not only applicable to assimilations and interactions with carbohydrates, but also more broadly (for example, with proteins[66], several micronutrients like calcium[67], or even fibers[68]).

Another interesting example can be illustrated by the following discoveries: while it is known that antioxidants, often abundant in fruits and vegetables, are often associated with significant health benefits (particularly through their actions against free radicals and oxidative stress, helping to preserve the health of our cells), several studies[69] have linked antioxidant supplementation in the form of

---

[65] *Ibid.*

[66] Boirie Y., Dangin M., Gachon P. et al. (1997). Slow and fast dietary proteins differently modulate postprandial protein accretion. *Proceedings of the National Academy of Sciences*, 94(26): 14930-5. https://doi.org/10.1073/pnas.94.26.14930

[67] Klobukowski J.A., Skibniewska K.A., Kowalski I.M. (2014). Calcium bioavailability from dairy products and its release from food by in vitro digestion. *Journal of Elementology*, 19(1):277-88, https://doi.org/10.5601/jelem.2014.19.1.436

[68] Fardet A. (2016). Do the physical structure and physicochemical characteristics of dietary fibers influence their health effects?. In: Hosseinian F, Oomah B.D., Campos-Vega R. *Dietary fibre functionality in food & nutraceuticals: From Plant to Gut*. John Wiley & Sons: Hoboken.

[69] Bjelakovic G., Nikolova D., Simonetti R.G., Gluud C. (2005). Antioxidant supplements for prevention of gastrointestinal cancers. *The Lancet*, Volume 365, Issue 9458, 471-472, https://doi.org/10.1016/S0140-6736(05)17858-1 ; Bjelakovic G., Nikolova D., Gluud C. (2014). Antioxidant supplements and mortality. *Current opinion in clinical nutrition and metabolic care,* 17(1), 40–44, https://doi.org/10.1097/MCO.0000000000000009 ; Bjelakovic G., Nikolova D., Gluud L.L., Simonetti R.G., Gluud C. (2012). Antioxidant supplements for prevention of mortality in healthy participants and patients with various diseases. *Cochrane*

dietary supplements (thus separated from their original matrices) not only to inefficiency in terms of prevention but worse, to potential excess mortality.

It is very likely that the fact that our bodies have an optimal interaction with foods according to their original matrices is the result of evolution, or in other words, the adaptation of our bodies to consume them in this way for tens of thousands of years.

I would like to emphasize that the example given about the apple does not necessarily imply that any alteration of a food matrix is always bad. It would be certainly incorrect and unfortunate to conclude that any transformation of a matrix would always spoil the health potential of the food. For example, olive oil, obtained after processes of transforming olives (extraction, pressing), can have potentially interesting health effects, not necessarily inferior to olives. Similarly, applesauce and apple juice are not strictly "bad for health."

However, it is fundamental, in order to understand the links between food and health, to conceive what the food matrix represents and the issues related to the matrix effect. **Ignorance of these facts can lead to a general misunderstanding of the effects of nutrition on health, erroneously thinking, for example, that the health potential of foods only depends on their quantitative nutritional values or nutrient compositions.**

This is still a widespread conception, which some call "nutritionism,"[70] not unrelated to the history of modern sciences. These sciences have indeed evolved towards a certain hegemony of

---

Database   *of*   *Systematic*   *Reviews,* https://doi.org/10.1002/14651858.CD007176.pub2

[70] Scrinis G. (2013). *Nutritionism - the science and politics of dietary advice.* Columbia University Press, New York.

quantitative calculations, sometimes at the expense of understanding certain qualitative properties[71].

But why are the food matrix and the matrix effect so important to conceive what healthy eating is? Simply because, most likely due to the fact that these concepts and this reality were not known, **for more than sixty years now, we have been accustomed to consuming degraded or even destroyed matrices. The industrialization of food, the evolution of technical, technological, and chemical processes of production, preservation, and distribution have led to the normalization of consuming foods that have been so transformed that they have become harmful to our health. This evolution temporally coincides with the rise in the prevalence of chronic diseases. These products now have a designation: they are called ultra-processed foods.**

Ultra-processing, or the degradation of food and human health

Ultra-processed foods, although present in our diets since the mid-20th century, have only recently been identified as such. They have been precisely termed since the creation of the NOVA food classification system[72], which distinguishes foods into four categories of processing.

---

[71] Quantitative data and complex calculations are always impressive and often serve as a guarantee of "scientificity" (although, obviously, they are useful and sometimes even indispensable for understanding various phenomena), but they are not worth much when their interpretations do not take into account certain qualitative properties.

[72] Monteiro C.A. et al. (2016). Food classification Public health, NOVA. The star shines bright. *World Nutrition*, Volume 7, Number 1, March 2016.

The first category refers to unprocessed or minimally processed foods, i.e., whole foods with no added ingredients, potentially undergoing moderate transformations (such as grinding, peeling, cooking, fermentation).

The second category, processed culinary ingredients, is typically used for cooking and seasoning. They are obtained through technical processes like pressing, grinding, drying, milling, or refining. Examples of processed culinary ingredients include sugar, salt, vegetable oils like olive oil or coconut oil, vinegar, spices, or broth[73].

The third category is that of processed foods: relatively simple products made by adding sugar, oil, salt, or other ingredients to raw foods. Most processed foods contain between two and five ingredients.

The fourth category is that of "ultra-processed" foods. These generally contain more than five ingredients, often including those found in processed foods (such as sugar, oils, fats, salt), as well as additives like flavors, stabilizers, or preservatives. Components found only in ultra-processed products include substances[74] not commonly used in culinary ingredients, aiming to mimic their sensory qualities or those of unprocessed foods[75].

Examples of ultra-processed foods include "soft drinks, sweet or savory packaged snacks, ice cream, industrial biscuits and cakes, candies, industrially produced bread and pastries, spreads, industrial breakfast cereals and 'energy' bars, energy drinks, milk-based drinks, 'fruit' yogurts and 'fruit' drinks, infant formulas, 'health' and 'slimming' products like dietary supplements, most ready-to-reheat pre-cooked meals, pies and prepared pasta dishes, industrial pizzas, poultry and fish nuggets and sticks, sausages, industrial hamburgers and hot dogs, and other reconstituted meat products, industrial soups, ready-to-reheat noodle dishes, as well as

---

[73] Fardet A. (2017). La classification NOVA : degré de transformation des aliments et santé. Université d'été de Nutrition, Centre de Recherche en Nutrition Humaine (CRNH). Clermont-Ferrand, France. (hal-01697078).

[74] Substances such as highly processed fats and proteins, additives, and flavors derived from food fractionation or chemical synthesis.

[75] Including taste, color, aroma, and texture.

powdered desserts."[76] Products undergoing drastic technological processes applied directly to raw foods, such as extrusion cooking or puffing (which disrupt the matrices of the concerned foods), as well as products containing cosmetic additives (like colorants), are also considered ultra-processed.

Ultra-processed products can be likened to foods that have been so heavily transformed that their matrices have been completely degraded and artificialized, even destroyed, such as nutrients or food fragments extracted from their matrix and then combined with other residues.

In this sense, **artificially extracted and recombined nutrients that partially compose certain ultra-processed foods are comparable to pieces of organisms, dead or dying, bearing little resemblance to their original state, incapable of nourishing us properly.** They also represent what is commonly referred to as "empty calories." While their quantities may remain the same, their quality and potential positive effects on the body are at best significantly reduced or nonexistent, and at worst, of negative value.

It is therefore possible to assert that ultra-processed foods, with matrices that have been too degraded or destroyed, are harmful to health. Both due to the presence of numerous additives and the degradation of matrices: our bodies are not adapted to their digestion and assimilation. **Ultra-processed foods are veritable bombs for chronic diseases!**

Increasingly, many epidemiological studies (about 200 to this day) link ultra-processed foods not only to chronic diseases in general but also to the development of several of them (including obesity, type-2 diabetes, cardiovascular diseases, certain cancers, chronic joint pathologies, and autoimmune diseases).

---

[76] Fardet A. (2017). *Halte aux aliments ultra-transformés*. Vergèze, Thierry Soucard Éditions.

A bit of epistemological knowledge and a pronounced critical mindset may lead us to the idea that most of these studies are quantitative research that, often by comparing the consumption of ultra-processed foods on one side and the prevalence of certain chronic diseases on the other, may incorrectly construct correlations between ultra-processed foods and the development of chronic diseases. Such reflection is not without relevance, considering, as we have seen before, chronic diseases are essentially multifactorial. It would be incorrect to attribute a single cause to them.

However, it would be absurd to claim, by supporting this type of reasoning, that there is no concrete evidence that ultra-processed foods are harmful to health.

Historical detours, epistemological biases, and a critical look at some nutritional recommendations

The type of critical reasoning outlined above, given as an example, remains important both in substance and form. While it may theoretically (albeit erroneously) question the relevance of labeling ultra-processed foods as harmful, **it also helps understand certain epistemological biases commonly made in nutrition and health sciences.**[77] **This requires a brief detour through the history of nutrition and its evolution as an academic discipline.**

Although it is challenging to pinpoint a precise and definitive origin, we know that nutrition has existed for a long time. At least since ancient Greece, through medieval Europe, it was practiced by physicians, holding a significant place in society concerning individuals' health[78]. In ancient and medieval societies, nutrition

---

[77] The approach is not to claim that I am more knowledgeable than the researchers who may have committed what I identify here as biases, but to allow myself to express a critical reasoning that, I think, can bring a certain added value.

[78] Drouard A. (2007). Perspectives historiques sur la notion de nutrition. Dans Audoin-Rouzea Frédérique et Sabban Françoise (dir), *Un aliment sain dans un corps sain – perspectives historiques*, Tours, Presses universitaires François Rabelais.

was inseparable from medicine and was not considered a specific discipline but part of the overall "science"[79] of health.

Some historians attribute the emergence of nutrition as a specialized science to a similar timeline as chemistry, partly thanks to Antoine Lavoisier (1743-1794). This progress continued with the work of Jean Trémolières (1913-1976), who marked "*a rupture in the history of human nutrition.*"[80] This physician and biologist defined nutrition as a "*coordinated application of biochemistry, cellular and general physiology, bacteriology, genetics, medicine, and agronomy to the improvement of nutrition, health, and the psycho-socio-economic values dependent on it.*"[81]

In the early 20th century, nutrition was not seen as a specialized discipline but as a combination and synthesis of existing knowledge for the overall optimization of nutrition for health[82]. Trémolières envisioned nutrition as a science of humanity, considering it in a holistic perspective, describing food as a human activity with multiple dimensions, including social aspects (referring to health problems related to food as "diseases of savoir-vivre", or lifestyle diseases).

However, after Trémolières' death in 1976, this comprehensive view of nutrition, focusing on all behaviors related to food for a general understanding, was deemed too ambitious and abandoned by his successors in favor of research that prioritizes physiological analysis. **Nutrition began to focus on its physicochemical aspects, particularly the study of what constitutes foods: nutrients. This**

---

[79] Whose etymology comes from the Latin "Scientia", originally referring to knowledge and its pursuit, and not the act of publishing in scientific journals with anonymous peer review evaluations.

[80] *Ibid.*

[81] Trémolières J. (1971). *Qu'est-ce que la nutrition ?* Paris, Ronéo.

[82] Audoin-Rouzeau F., Sabban F. (2007). *Un aliment sain dans un corps sain – perspectives historiques, op.cit.*

focus directed nutrition toward increased knowledge production about what nutrients are.

In parallel, health sciences evolved under a certain quantitative and mathematical hegemony[83], notably with the advent of epidemiology in the 20th century[84]. Epidemiology, through quantitative studies on cohorts of individuals or populations, determines correlations between certain factors and alterations or maintenance of health in the subjects studied. These correlations contribute to establishing probable cause-and-effect relationships between negative factors (negatively influencing health) or positive factors.

For approximately 70 years, it has been the convergence of these two disciplines, "nutritional epidemiology," that legitimately determines what is good or bad for health. Public health recommendations regarding nutrition are primarily formulated based on nutritional epidemiology.

I am well aware that these historical and contextual detours may have seemed tedious and somewhat off-topic compared to my approach. However, they are crucial to know and consider because they help understand certain biases and inaccuracies in our modern representations of the links between food and health.

The epistemological problem is as follows: by relying on knowledge produced in nutrition (focused on nutrient studies), nutritional epidemiology has determined cause-and-effect relationships between food and health, sometimes inaccurately but legitimized

---

[83] This term is not used in a pejorative sense. It is rather an observation: nowadays, the legitimacy and validity of a treatment, or the recognition of an agent as pathogenic, rely on the need to have «proved» it through quantitative studies (involving correlations and potential cause-and-effect relationships demonstrated by mathematical calculations).

[84] Schlienger J.L. (2022). Petite histoire de l'épidémiologie de l'Antiquité à nos jours. *Médecine des Maladies Métaboliques*, Volume 16, Issue 2, 2022, P. 191-199, ISSN 1957-2557, https://doi.org/10.1016/j.mmm.2021.11.006

in collective representations, notably through rigorous mathematical calculations.

These associations, centered on quantitative correlations and nutrients, have not integrated certain qualitative properties, such as the importance of the food matrix and the reality of the matrix effect. This resulted in attributing "good" or "bad" characteristics to nutrients themselves.

Certainly, I do not claim that this knowledge is worthless or unimportant, but it seems fundamental to understand the implications that such a history may have had on our conceptions of nutrition and on current recommendations.

This "deconstruction" partially helps us better understand why, despite the proliferation of nutritional recommendations for more than forty years, chronic diseases, including obesity and type-2 diabetes, have not regressed[85]. I propose to revisit some common misconceptions and address them within Box No. 3.

---

[85] And it is possible to posit that, even if the recommendations had been followed to the letter, it is not certain that significant positive effects on health would have ensued.

"Dietary fibers are good for health" (or "for your health, consume more dietary fibers").

Understanding such a statement and health recommendation requires, once again, conceptualizing how we arrived at this conclusion. I will attempt to explain this by simplifying and vulgarizing extreme examples of steps that lead to it:

1. Multiple data on a panel of 20,000 individuals, including their health status and dietary habits, are available.

2. Several categories are distinguished within this panel regarding individuals' health status: those in good health (without pathology), those who are obese, and those who are obese and have another chronic disease.

3. The "variables" (health status and dietary habits) are cross-referenced, revealing significant mathematically meaningful correlations.

4. As commonly done in nutritional epidemiology, dietary habits are distinguished based on differences in ingested nutrients.

5. It is observed that individuals in good health consume more fiber-rich foods.

6. It is concluded that there is likely a cause-and-effect relationship between regular fiber consumption and good health.

7. Thanks to the scientific legitimacy and significance of the study's calculations, recommendations are made to consume fiber-rich foods and "fiber," and public opinion incorporates the idea that "dietary fibers are good for health."

Of course, these examples are extremely simplified, and the reality of research in nutritional epidemiology is much more complex. **The problem is that by focusing on nutrients composing foods, we assert that it is the fibers themselves that are good for health, not the foods containing them.**

The stakes are significant because this could allow agro-food companies to artificially inflate the fiber content of their products, selling them as

"healthy" because they contain "a lot of fiber." However, an understanding of the matrix effect and the qualitative degradation of nutrients when extracted from their matrix makes us aware that **such ultra-processed products with high fiber content are very unlikely, if not strictly impossible, to be good for health.**

Furthermore, it helps us understand that it is probably not the fibers themselves that are good for health, but the foods that are naturally rich in fibers. This proposal, developed by combining logic, qualitative properties (matrix effect), and the example of quantitative study steps given above, may be considered by some as "unscientific" precisely because it does not result from a published quantitative study evaluated through peer review. This represents, in my opinion, a significant limitation regarding the modern production of knowledge and the variability of its legitimacy depending on the method employed—although it is not the core of the subject here.

The same type of explanation that I formulated for fibers can be applied to similar biases:

"Antioxidants are good for health."

It is highly probable that this kind of reasoning, following the examples of steps proposed earlier, led to the idea that "antioxidants are good for health," then prompted some pharmaceutical companies to produce and some practitioners to prescribe antioxidants as dietary supplements. Applying the logic of the matrix effect, I refer again to the studies mentioned earlier indicating that antioxidant supplements have not been associated with health benefits (but rather the opposite).

Let's now focus on the idea that:

"Sugar is bad for health" (and its alternatives: "For your health, limit sugar consumption"; "avoid eating too much sugar," etc.).

Here, it is necessary, once again, to **distinguish "free" or refined sugar—extracted from the original food or plant matrices (whether sugar cane, beets, or fruits)—from naturally sweet foods eaten within their original matrix.** Integrating the reality of the matrix effect into the reasoning allows us to understand that it is not sugar or carbohydrates that are inherently bad for health, but rather sugars extracted from their original matrices (to be added to products)[86].

If we do not consider the matrix effect and rely on the quantitative-related idea that one should "limit sugar consumption" or "limit sugary products," **it may lead us to merely count the carbohydrate levels of the foods we consume, without considering their degree of transformation. According to this logic, ingesting twenty strawberries (about 16g of carbohydrates) would be equivalent to eating 4 and a half *TAGADA* strawberries (about 16g of carbohydrates)!**

However, it is evident that these two types of foods have nothing to do with each other. The consumption of strawberries tends to have a positive interaction with the body[87], while the consumption of ultra-processed sweets composed of free sugars and several chemicals and additives is likely to trigger a negative reaction in the body.

The ingestion of naturally sweet foods, rich in carbohydrates, is not harmful as part of a balanced diet, as carbohydrates are essential energy sources for the proper functioning and development of our bodies, brains, and cells. Naturally sweet foods are usually composed of other essential and positive nutrients (when eaten within their matrix), making their consumption as whole foods generally beneficial for maintaining good health. **(There is even talk of "nutrient synergy", to describe the fact that nutrients interact optimally with the body when absorbed together in their matrix.)**

---

[86] Fardet A., Rock E. (2022). Chronic diseases are first associated with the degradation and artificialization of food matrices rather than with food composition: calorie quality matters more than calorie quantity. *European journal of nutrition*, 61(5), 2239–2253. https://doi.org/10.1007/s00394-021-02786-8

[87] Ovied-Solís C.I., Cornejo-Manzo S., Murillo-Ortiz B.O., Guzmán-Barrón M.M., Ramírez-Emiliano J. (2018). Los polifenoles de la fresa disminuyen el estrés oxidativo en enfermedades crónicas [Strawberry polyphenols decrease oxidative stress in chronic diseases]. *Gaceta medica de Mexico*, 154(1), 80–86. https://doi.org/10.24875/GMM.17002759 ; Giampieri F., Forbes-Hernandez T.Y., Gasparrini M., Afrin S., Cianciosi D., Reboredo-Rodriguez P., Varela-Lopez A., Quiles J.L., Mezzetti B., Battino M. (2017). The healthy effects of strawberry bioactive compounds on molecular pathways related to chronic diseases. *Annals of the New York Academy of Sciences*, 1398(1), 62–71. https://doi.org/10.1111/nyas.13373

While ultra-processed artificially sweetened foods have almost no advantages[88] but rather disadvantages (hormonal and metabolic dysregulations, inflammations, and disruptions in the microbiota that, accumulated over the long term, pave the way for the development of several chronic diseases).

Once again, recommendations like "limiting sugary products" need to be reconsidered when integrating the importance of the food matrix and the matrix effect: **it is not "sugary products" that are bad for health[89] but artificially sweetened products (with sugars extracted from their matrix), unlike naturally sweet foods that are not**.

I propose presenting eating "real" and whole foods as the first axis defining the basics of a healthy diet. This also implies asserting that **the quality of nutrients and calories is more important than their quantity,** mainly depending on their matrix quality, as **"the matrix governs nutrients."** [90]

By transposing these ideas negatively, it also leads to the statement that **consuming foods whose matrix has been too degraded or destroyed is generally not healthy: that is the case for ultra-processed foods**.

I take care to specify "generally" here because these are trend truths ("eating healthily involves eating foods whose matrices have not been degraded") that may involve some very rare exceptions.

---

[88] One can always argue that carbohydrates, even when free (extracted from their matrix), still provide "energy". This remains debatable in my opinion when considering the fact that digestion itself is energy-consuming, and empty calories (dead or dying nutrients extracted from their matrices and degraded, like organs removed from their bodies), offering little in terms of caloric quality, will likely cost the body more energy during digestion than they provide.

[89] Although a diet primarily based on naturally sweet real foods would still probably be detrimental in the long run, as it would be unbalanced and too high in carbohydrates.

[90] Fardet A., Rock E. (2022). Chronic diseases are first associated with the degradation and artificialization of food matrices rather than with food composition: calorie quality matters more than calorie quantity. *op.cit.*

Debates are ongoing about how much daily intake of calories from ultra-processed foods is possible without affecting our health. **I personally think it is prudent, even urgent, to completely and definitively stop their consumption (considering that we do not know all the effects they may have over the very long term or across several generations)**.

This idea may seem radical, but I do not intend to encourage consuming, let alone ingesting, something "in moderation," knowing this is inherently harmful (and brings nothing good, except for an apparent "economic" aspect that does not consider its hidden costs—a semblance of pleasure that only deceives our taste buds and our brains).

In fact, it is probably more urgent to be fully aware of these parameters when considering the links between food and health. It is precisely because they are still poorly known and poorly understood at the present time that I deemed it essential to take the time to develop my argument and presentation regarding the importance of eating whole foods.

Second Axis: Eating a balanced and varied diet (provided it's based on whole foods)

I won't need to elaborate as much on the interest of a balanced diet, as it is already a universally recognized fact[91] with numerous recommendation campaigns circulating for some time. However, I deem it crucial to provide some general clarifications on this matter and express my opinion on currently controversial issues.

The absolute importance of eating real food does not negate the significance of a balanced diet. In other words, the understanding of the food matrix and the matrix effect, along with the epistemological critiques I've raised regarding quantitative

---

[91] One often hears about a "balanced diet," confused with the concept of a healthy diet (at least in France).

tendencies and potential biais in nutritional epidemiology, should not be misconstrued as an attempt to discard more than seven decades of research.

Modern nutrition, focusing on the study of nutrients, and nutritional epidemiology have merit in helping us better comprehend our general nutrient requirements—essentially, understanding the quantities of nutrients needed for good health.

Following the logic of my argument, I emphasize that a balanced diet, for good health, involves not only meeting our nutritional needs but satisfying these needs through the consumption of real and whole foods. The question of balance and nutritional needs becomes fundamental and intriguing only once we understand that nutrient quality depends on the quality of their matrix (or, in simpler terms, once ultra-processed foods are eliminated from our diet).

Conversely, prioritizing nutritional needs over eating real food, not only fails to align with a healthy diet but can also lead to numerous pitfalls. For instance, one might sell ultra-processed foods, where nutrients have lost much of their matrix quality, along with chemical endocrine disruptors (sweeteners, preservatives, artificial or natural[92] flavors, colorings, etc.), claiming they are "good for health" because they help "satisfy all our nutritional needs." This practice is both an absurdity and a commercial deception, misleading consumers into thinking they are eating healthily by consuming a "balanced" products.

Once real and whole foods are part of the equation, the consideration of balance becomes crucial. It helps us better understand the compositions of what we ingest and ensures that we avoid deficiencies or overconsumption of certain nutrients[93].

---

[92] Which actually has little that is natural (or in this case, "everything is natural," since it inevitably has a distant natural origin).

[93] Significant imbalances, including deficiencies such as in proteins and essential amino acids, or overconsumption, for example, in carbohydrates, can play a role in the development of various health issues, sometimes substantial, but maybe not to

Nutrition and nutritional epidemiology have revealed the roles of carbohydrates, fats, proteins, fibers, vitamins, and minerals in our daily lives, affecting our immune system, cognition, brain activity, cell function, muscle development, growth, etc.

These needs are not universal in terms of quantities, although overall averages and minimum requirements can be established. They vary among individuals and depend on various parameters such as size, weight, and morphology, age, physical activity, energy expenditure, daily activities, genetics, ethnic origins, life goals, etc. This book is not a nutrition manual, which is why I will refrain from providing specific examples regarding different nutritional needs based on one's profile and these various parameters.

However, we will note the idea that nutritional needs are not the same for all individuals, and consequently, it is not relevant to conceive of an absolutely universal and optimal balance that could be recommended to everyone. This is not a relativistic proposition, which would claim that there are no common rules regarding nutritional needs: because **everyone can be deficient, especially in proteins and lipids[94], vitamins, minerals, or other micronutrients, or even overconsume certain nutrients[95].**

So, eating a balanced diet will involve, at a technically more advanced level than that required for eating whole, being able to identify and know one's needs for lipids, proteins, carbohydrates (etc.) based on one's daily energy needs and profile. This does not mean that any carbohydrate is equivalent to any other carbohydrate (which is true for each of the nutrient categories). Not only are

---

the extent that ultra-processed foods have done over the past seventy years for the entire population.

[94] The question of carbohydrate deficiencies remains controversial, as it is not impossible to drastically reduce carbohydrate consumption without necessarily being in a poor state of health (especially in the short term, although this is debatable in the long term).

[95] Like carbohydrates, to which our bodies are not adapted for excessive consumption, even when ingested through high-quality foods.

carbohydrates from ultra-processed foods not equivalent (qualitatively, and therefore in their interactions with the body) to carbohydrates from whole foods, but also, even within two different whole foods, not all carbohydrates are equal, and this, for at least two reasons:

1) Carbohydrates are a category of nutrients, within which more specifically fall monosaccharides (glucose), disaccharides (sucrose, lactose), polysaccharides (starch, glycogen, cellulose...) (each of them having its own physiological properties and interacting differently with the body); 2) Carbohydrates exist only within food matrices. This implies that the glucose in an apple is not exactly the same as that in a banana, because the two fruits are two different organisms.

These specificities and distinctions have, in my opinion, two major consequences.

Firstly, due to the technicality that the knowledge and understanding of nutrients require (multiple complex appellations, specific physicochemical properties to study, etc.): **in the context of food education, learning about nutrients, as a specific and complex approach to the links between food and health, should occur later and at a higher level than the study of the food matrix and the matrix effect (as a qualitative and simple approach to the links between diet and health)**. It is undoubtedly always more consistent and practical to go from the more general and simple to the more specific and complex.

Secondly, and particularly due to the fact that a category of nutrients does not imply equivalence in quality and content within several foods containing the same amount, **it appears much more delicate and risky than it may seem to replace one food with another, due to its same content in a certain quantity of nutrients**.

I will give a rather controversial and current example: namely, **the idea that, in order to meet daily and weekly protein needs, it is equivalent in its effects on the body to ingest the same number of** grams of protein through the consumption of meat, fish, or eggs as through those contained in plant-based proteins.

This proposition is often brought up and highlighted in arguments extolling the virtues of a vegetarian diet (or its alternatives that strongly encourage reducing, if not completely stopping, the consumption of meat or even all animal products).

However, it can be criticized[96], which implies delving more into what proteins are and their roles for our bodies. Without going into the detail and comprehensiveness of their biological compositions, proteins are primarily composed of amino acids (the assembly of which forms a protein). They play a fundamental role in the health of our cells (especially for the immune system, or growth and maintenance of muscular, skeletal, capillary, and cutaneous tissues) as well as for our overall health.

Protein interactions with our bodies depend on their essential amino acid content and digestibility. A score (**DIAAS**) has been established to show how essential amino acid levels and their digestibility[97] vary among proteins in different foods. For example, at equal protein quantity, animal products like chicken breast (1.08) and eggs (1.13) receive DIAAS scores about twice as high as soy tofu (0.52), almonds (0.40), or green peas (0.58)[98] (plant-based sources known for their high protein content). **Thus, animal products, including meat, fish, and eggs, provide proteins more than twice as rich and digestible in essential amino acids as plant-based sources, including those with the highest protein content.**

---

[96] It is not my intention here to criticize the ethical and ideological foundations of vegetarian movements, but rather, from a entirely pragmatic perspective, to deconstruct the idea that all proteins are equal and have the same effects on the body.

[97] Without taking into account anti-nutrients that are found in plant-based foods.

[98] Phillips S.M. (2017). Current Concepts and Unresolved Questions in Dietary Protein Requirements and Supplements in Adults. *Frontiers in Nutrition*, 4. https://doi.org/10.3389/fnut.2017.00013

This doesn't mean that animal products are necessarily and always "superior" to plant-based ones. Nevertheless, qualities (qualitative properties) cannot be attributed to foods based on scores (quantitative properties), due to logical reasons. However, we can understand that foods cannot substitute for each other solely based on nutrient needs (or even minimal needs).

Each food and food type contributes different elements to the body, emphasizing that "eating balanced" consistently involves diversifying one's diet, or in other words, "eating varied." I would complete the phrase with "eating varied, and everything that contributes to meeting our nutritional needs."

Firstly, variety helps achieve balance in the sense that balance should not focus on ensuring we ingest enough—and not too much—fats, proteins, carbohydrates (etc.), but enough different and varied real foods that, through their diversity, provide balance and fulfill these needs. Secondly, **variety brings additional, significant richness to nourish our microbiota, which plays a crucial role in our health and immune system**.

Eating balanced and varied thus implies diversifying the foods consumed to maximize the chances of meeting nutritional needs and providing energetic and bacterial richness to the body, considering all the foods and food groups that our species has been accustomed to consuming as omnivores.

Therefore, to gain a deeper understanding of our nutritional and dietary needs, **it is essential to integrate that these needs are inherently linked to evolution[99]: the dietary behaviors of our ancestors, which, through prolonged heritability, conditioned the functioning of our bodies and their needs to ensure activities that keep them alive and in good health** (characteristics that can differ

---

[99] Leonard W.R., Roberton M.L. (1992). Nutritional Requirement and Human Evolution: a Bioenergetics Model. *American journal of human biology*, 4: 179-195. https://doi.org/10.1002/ajhb.1310040204

among regions worldwide and ethnic origins, hence not completely universal).

Of course, I don't express this idea based on "traditionalism" or any ideology, but rather to pragmatically approach the risks that can result from abrupt disruptions in the time of consuming a food or food type compared to one's ancestors and hundreds of thousands of years of evolution[100].

The primary risk is that it may lead to deficiencies and, consequently, nutritional imbalance. After all, we are not omnivores[101] for nothing!

---

[100] This is also true for the risk associated with any increased consumption of foods or products that our ancestors, especially distant ones, never consumed. In the short term, I am obviously referring to ultra-processed foods and xenobiotics or additives that our bodies are not adapted to digest. But over a longer period, we can once again question the fact that agriculture is relatively recent in comparison to the history of human evolution, implying a significant disruption in dietary practices over the last 12,000 years (including a significant increase in the consumption of cereals, and more generally, a substantial rise in carbohydrate intake). This kind of reasoning leads us to consider that nutrition remains a young science, and that various nutritional recommendations can sometimes be criticized, given the difficulty of arriving at precise knowledge of our nutrient needs considering these multiple parameters (taking into account the lifestyles of our distant ancestors, limitations related to conclusions drawn from quantitative epidemiological studies, etc.). All of this does not make things any less complicated. The concept of balance is indeed a technical and advanced aspect of nutrition.

[101] The acidity of the human stomach, as a product of evolution, has been observed to be approximately in the middle, between that of carnivores and herbivores (although still closer to carnivores), thus showing us that evolution has conditioned us (in that our bodies are designed to match the behaviors of our ancestors) to be omnivores. See: Beasley D.E., Koltz A.M., Lambert J.E., Fierer N., Dunn R.R. (2015). The Evolution of Stomach Acidity and Its Relevance to the Human Microbiome. *PLoS One*, 10(7): e0134116. https://doi.org/10.1371/journal.pone.0134116

Box No. 4: "For your health, reduce your meat consumption"

You probably understood that I am referring, among other things, to the risks of deficiencies posed, for example, by diets in which one decides to completely or significantly eliminate all animal products or meat. **It is true that meat consumption, especially red meat, has a somewhat bad reputation**[102] **these days, increasingly associated in scientific literature and, especially, in public health campaigns, with the risks of developing chronic pathologies and diseases**[103].

In this regard, and for the sake of coherence and accuracy, I would like to suggest that it is again possible to apply the same type of criticism that I have constructed earlier. These studies, mostly still in nutritional epidemiology, seem to me to have a **major bias of considering "meat" (or "red meat") as a single category: that is, without making qualitative distinctions, which are nonetheless significant!**

For example, it is neither fair nor accurate to consider in the same way an industrial beef piece from intensive farming, where the animal has been pumped with antibiotics, poorly nourished and mistreated, and which will be served in a fast-food[104] sandwich with additives; ultra-processed deli meat (enriched with nitrites, dextrose, colorings, and other chemical delights); and a steak from high-quality farming, where the animal lived in decent conditions (food, outdoor life, animal well-being). **It goes without**

---

[102] Not to mention issues that do not concern human health (which I will not address in this book).

[103] As I have already introduced the idea, although fruits are associated with several health benefits, excessive (or unlimited) consumption of fruits is not healthy. It constitutes an overconsumption of certain carbohydrates and may play a role in increasing blood sugar levels and developing insulin resistance. However, it would not come to mind to generally associate "fruits" with type-2 diabetes or human fatty liver disease (as is done, however, for meat and certain chronic diseases). It is, in this sense, important to understand the importance of balance, which allows seeking a middle ground or a proper measure in the ingestion of different types of foods.

[104] Yes, eating meat in a fast-food restaurant, which is likely to come from intensive farming (with all that it implies), does not have the same effects on health as eating high-quality, genuine meat from qualitative farming.

saying that these three types of red meat will have absolutely different effects on the body!

By lumping together these three very different products under a single category of "red meat," it does not seem, both in substance and in form, appropriate to conclude that "red meat" constitutes a risk for chronic diseases[105].

The bias can persist even in health recommendations derived from this kind of study, in the tone of "for your health, reduce your red meat consumption." We might wonder if this type of recommendation is truly coherent on a health level when addressed universally. Is it genuinely beneficial for their health to communicate this kind of message to individuals who are already close to being vegetarians (and potentially deficient in essential amino acids or constrained to dietary supplementations)?

Indeed, while **it is theoretically possible to survive** by substituting proteins from animal products with proteins from plant products to meet the average minimum protein and essential amino acid needs of a human[106], **it is based precisely on calculations established on average minimum needs[107], and not optimal needs.** That is, without considering individual specificities in essential amino acid needs, which vary, especially depending on one's physical activity.

For example, **engaging in muscle-development exercises or intense physical activity, requiring frequent repair of numerous muscle fibers to**

---

[105] In this regard, the study by Lescinsky et al., which focused on the health effects of unprocessed red meat, concluded that the evidence of an association between it and the development of chronic diseases is too weak and insufficient to draw recommendations (to limit its consumption): see Lescinsky H., Afshin A., Ashbaugh C., Bisignano C., Brauer M., Ferrara G., Hay S.I., He J., Iannucci V., Marczak L.B., McLaughlin S.A., Mullany E.C., Parent M.C., Serfes A.L., Sorensen R.J.D., Aravkin A.Y., Zheng P., Murray C.J.L. (2022). Health effects associated with consumption of unprocessed red meat: a Burden of Proof study. *Nature Medicine*, 28(10), 2075–2082. https://doi.org/10.1038/s41591-022-01968-z

[106] Mariotti F., Gardner C.D. (2019). Dietary Protein and Amino Acids in Vegetarian Diets-A Review. *Nutrients*, 11(11), 2661. https://doi.org/10.3390/nu11112661

[107] Carbone J.W., Pasiakos S.M. (2019). Dietary Protein and Muscle Mass: Translating Science to Application and Health Benefit. *Nutrients*, 11(5), 1136. https://doi.org/10.3390/nu11051136

a varying degree, demands substantial daily intake of essential amino acids, higher than for someone who does not engage in such activities[108]. These needs can quickly become challenging to fulfill by completely avoiding animal products[109].

It seems very risky, therefore, to establish an absolute cause-and-effect relationship between "meat," as a category without any distinction in quality, and poor health, by universally advocating for its reduction.

To delve deeper into the critique and extension of this reasoning, universally encouraging a reduction in animal product consumption, based on the assumption that we can satisfy our minimum average needs for essential amino acids solely through plant products, would, in fact, imply a general reduction (on average) in physical activity (to avoid raising essential amino acid needs). This could also imply the impossibility of increasing physical activity intensity[110]. Considering how fundamental both nutrition and physical activity are to maintaining good health, it seems reasonable to adopt a critical stance towards this type of proposition.

Let's be clear: I absolutely do not intend to take a "pro-meat" position or an inherently "anti-vegetarianism" stance, even less so based on ideology. My argumentation is not affiliated with any particular values or militant position (it is important to emphasize this fact). Vegetarians likely have multiple legitimate reasons for their choices[111].

---

[108] *Ibid.*; Ciuris C., Lynch H.M., Wharton C., Johnston C.S. (2019). A Comparison of Dietary Protein Digestibility, Based on DIAAS Scoring, in Vegetarian and Non-Vegetarian Athletes. *Nutrients*, 11(12):3016. https://doi.org/10.3390/nu11123016

[109] Alternatively, this implies supplementing with proteins (extracted and isolated from their matrices), or even with hormones, using products that are very often highly processed (including capsules) and harmful in the long term.

[110] One might respond here by mentioning several professional athletes known to be vegetarians. However, I would remain cautious about what this proves (or does not prove) since we have almost no hindsight regarding vegetarianism and its impact on the health of professional athletes. Anyone who has engaged in intense and regular physical activity knows how challenging it is to abstain from the consumption of any animal products, involving, among other things, a much more frequent meal intake or unnatural supplementation.

[111] In connection with this statement, it is in my opinion important to distinguish between so-called "environmental" issues and those related to human health. I encourage, in this regard, a reconsideration of the idea that we must "reduce our

On the other hand, it is noteworthy that excessive consumption of red meat can potentially be detrimental to health, specifically due to increased acidity and toxins it may contain. Hence, the importance of balance and varied eating!

The aim is to caution against potential health effects of depriving ourselves of foods or food categories that our bodies have been accustomed to ingesting over tens of thousands of years, considering that these habits are closely linked to our needs as omnivores.

Voluntarily abstaining from specific foods or types of foods that contribute to satisfying our needs should be done with a certain awareness of the risks it may entail, not with the goal of optimizing one's health.

Meeting our nutritional needs by eating a balanced and varied diet is, in this sense, very important, as it allows our bodies to function as they are conditioned to[112]. Eating balanced and varied promotes good functioning of our endocrine system (or hormone production) and, more generally, good health.

In conclusion of this second axis, we will emphasize that balance and variety are fundamental to aiming for a diet that is good for health. However, balance has no value if one has not previously become aware of the reality of the matrix effect. **More complex, more technical, and consequently more difficult to access, what is related to dietary balance and nutrients should logically, in the context of food education, be learned later than knowledge related to the matrix effect or in the chronological continuity of a curriculum.** Variety is a simpler dimension than balance, as it can

---

meat consumption" "for our health," to which significant nuances should be added (including a distinction between industrial animal products of poor quality and from intensive production, and high-quality animal products from sustainable farming; as well as a distinction between health and environmental issues, which do not intertwine as simply and easily as one tends to believe, following a simplistic logic of "meat = bad").

[112] In this sense, health is, in a way, closely linked to evolution, at least regarding nutrition.

theoretically be understood at any age, for example, through the discovery of new foods.

Third axis: Try to avoid pathogenic chemicals

Awareness of the multifactorial causes of chronic diseases requires a global perspective, aiming to maximize the chances of nourishing oneself by avoiding, as much as possible, each of them. This logically implies attempting to avoid ingesting pathogenic artificial chemicals[113].

Increased exposure to pathogenic chemicals, including those outside of food and water, is indeed recognized as a significant cause of the growth of chronic diseases. This position may seem controversial, as it presupposes a certain kind of reductionist and simplistic reasoning, such as "what is chemical is bad." The reality is, of course, more complex, partly because many "chemical" productions also contribute, in a way, to our good health[114].

However, all artificial chemicals contained in food are associated with negative health effects. This holds true for all food additives[115] found in most ultra-processed foods, as well as for residues of

---

[113] I am referring here to artificial chemical products (therefore derived from human production): that is, substances that do not exist as such in nature or have been produced by copying existing molecules. Thus, a chemical component (for example, a nutrient) is not a chemical product.

[114] Chemistry and the design of chemical molecules have played a significant role in the advancements in medicine, leading to a substantial reduction in the prevalence of communicable diseases during the 20th century.

[115] Lerner A. (2016). Multiple Food Additives Enhance Human Chronic Diseases. *SOJ Microbiology & Infectious Diseases*, 4. 01-02. https://doi.org/10.15226/sojmid/4/2/00149 ; Paula Neto H.A., Ausina P., Gomez L.S., Leandro J., Zancan P., Sola-Penna M. (2017). Effects of Food Additives on Immune Cells As Contributors to Body Weight Gain and Immune-Mediated Metabolic Dysregulation. *Frontiers in immunology*, 8, 1478. https://doi.org/10.3389/fimmu.2017.01478

artificial chemicals used in production, such as pesticides and various chemical fertilizers.

In fact, **the idea of linking "real food" to healthy eating extends to the process of food production** (both agriculture and livestock). **Productions using various artificial chemical agents to optimize yields also degrade the potential beneficial interactions of foods with the body and their overall quality.**

Therefore, eating real involves paying attention to the production conditions of food products, even in the case of non-ultra-processed foods. This applies to both plant and animal products (animal feed, living spaces, health treatments, etc.).

In the face of these challenges, organic farming and livestock could correspond to a healthier diet. The foods derived from them are produced according to a set of rules and requirements based on French or European Union labels, allowing them to be marketed and sold as "organic." They are theoretically and generally produced with fewer artificial chemicals than foods from so-called "conventional"[116] production. Similarly, for livestock, the conditions imposed to obtain the label seem quite strict, ensuring a minimum of well-being for the animals and a diet that is presumably non-pathogenic.

However, it seems important not to idealize the organic label too much and, above all, not to take it for what it is not.

Firstly, because French and European rules regarding organic labeling still allow the use of phytosanitary products (sometimes called "biopesticides"), which are supposed to be more natural than

---

[116] It is still quite incredible that intensive production, using numerous artificial chemical products, for which we now have all the evidence that they are harmful to both human health and the environment (soil pollution, water pollution, threats to animals and biodiversity, and to life in general), is still referred to as 'conventional' (due to its widespread use since the early 20th century, parallel to the rise of chronic diseases). The deterioration of the population's health is not, in fact, so surprising when such conventions are in use.

those used in so-called conventional agriculture. By consulting lists of authorized phytosanitary products in organic farming, it is observed that some of them are composed of products that appear to be relatively harmless (various oils and essential oils), but many others contain some chemicals known to be more or less harmful to health (iron phosphate, ethylene, pyrethrin, etc.).

Secondly, because **organic is a label related to the restriction of the use of pathogenic chemical agents during the agricultural production of food, which does not include controls or limitations on what will happen to the food afterward (after the agricultural production phase): hence the existence and presence in supermarkets of many ultra-processed organic foods**[117]. It is important to consider that eating organic does not necessarily mean eating more natural[118] and certainly not eating "real".

Thirdly, because organic farming and livestock may not be so incompatible with intensive and industrial production (for example, in Europe, organic eggs may come from farms with tens of thousands of hens, raising questions about how so many animals can simultaneously receive good treatment and quality food).

The organic label, however, represents a certain advantage, namely that, **when choosing among several types of real foods, those that are organic are more likely to have been produced with fewer artificial and pathogenic chemicals than non-organic ones.** However, these are only probabilities and not necessarily the reality on the ground, especially since many small, often local, producers

---

[117] Davidou S., Frank K., Christodoulou A., Fardet A. (2022). Organic food retailing: to what extent are foods processed and do they contain markers of ultra-processing ?. *International Journal of Food Sciences and Nutrition*, 73(2), p. 172-183. https://doi.org/10.1080/09637486.2021.1966395

[118] Not to mention the possibility of adding a few chemical products or additives to foods once they have passed their agricultural production phase, as exemplified by the inclusion of nitrites in many products labeled as organic.

grow without the use of pesticides and chemical fertilizers but do not always obtain the costly and sometimes debatable organic label.

Avoiding artificial chemical products in one's diet is not easy, and it is not always fully guaranteed by consuming organic products, which represent additional costs.

This is why I present this as the third axis of a healthy diet, as it is both simpler to eat real, then to eat balanced and varied, than to eat while avoiding ingesting harmful artificial chemical products (in practice, although simpler than eating balanced in theory).

Also, eating organic, in order to minimize contact with artificial chemical products, without first eating real and whole foods, and without eating balanced and varied, does not seem to have real health benefits. In the sense that it does not allow for a healthy diet, conducive to maintaining good health and contributing to the prevention of chronic diseases.

Conclusion on what constitutes a healthy diet

A real and whole foods based diet, balanced and varied, while attempting to avoid pathogenic chemicals and their residues, corresponds to a diet that is healthy for human health, contributing to maintaining good health and preventing chronic diseases.

These three main axes constitute the foundations for understanding the main challenges of the links between food and health. It aims to provide an accessible and easily understandable approach, trying to bring together the most important aspects within a coherent overall logic.

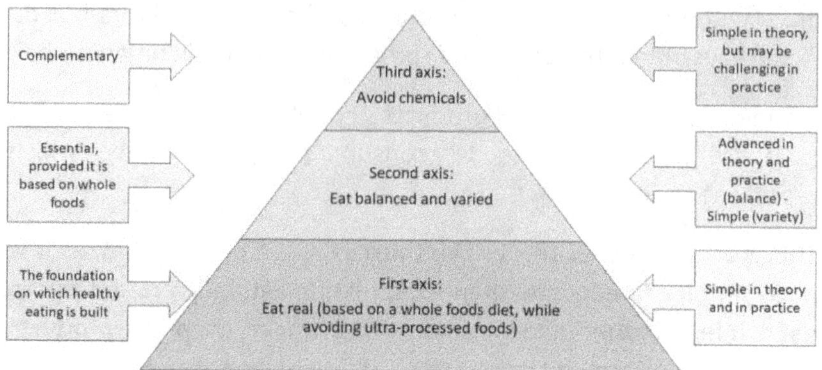

Figure No. 1: Three key axes to define what a healthy diet is

Eating real and whole foods serves as the foundation of a healthy diet, so if this axis is not considered and its application is neglected, the other two have very little interest. This dimension is simple in theory and practice because it does not require advanced knowledge of nutrition but merely an understanding of certain principles (food matrix, matrix effect, degrees of processing).

Eating balanced and varied is also an essential dimension for a healthy diet, on condition of being based on real and whole foods. Balance is crucial because it allows understanding one's nutrient needs, ensuring not to be deficient or overconsume certain nutrients.

For example, a protein deficiency can lead to a general weakening of the immune system and chronic fatigue, while an overconsumption of carbohydrates can, over time, promote the development of obesity or type 2 diabetes (although, once again, not all "carbohydrates" should be lumped together!).

Balance requires at least an "intermediate" level in theory and practice, as it involves studying nutrients and their complexity (categories of macronutrients and micronutrients, specific nutrients, effects on the body, etc.). Variety is more accessible than balance, contributing to it: all it takes is an interest in or exploration of new foods, learning about their origins, and understanding their specificities. Beyond balance, it is interesting and essential because it provides the body with nutritional, dietary, bacterial, and energy richness and diversity it needs to maintain good health.

I have combined the two dimensions, "eating balanced and varied," as they seem linked and complementary, so that balance without variety or variety without balance remains limited. However, it is important to note that variety represents an accessible means of promoting balance, for example, in the case of a young age or a lack of nutrition knowledge.

Eating while trying to avoid chemicals and their residues in one's diet is, in my opinion, a complementary aspect because this doesn't have much interest if one doesn't already eat "real", balanced, and varied. On the other hand, if one already considers and practices a whole foods based diet, balanced, varied, trying to avoid chemicals maximizes the chances of having a healthy diet by avoiding, as much as possible, chemical pollutants that act as endocrine disruptors and vectors of chronic diseases.

Although very simple in theory, practical difficulties involved, including additional costs that do not allow complete certainty of avoiding any direct or indirect contact with chemical pathogens, led me to conceive this axis as complementary and not as crucial as the first two.

I will again emphasize that this part does not claim to offer an exhaustive analysis of what is and is not a healthy diet. To do so, many other aspects would have deserved to be addressed, developed, and some that I already mention could have been further explored (such as the triangular relationship between diet, health, and the environment, or some of the ecological and environmental benefits of eating "real" and varied, which will subsequently impact human health, or the importance of seasonality and local consumption, allowing access to fresher and healthier foods with better-preserved matrix and nutrients qualities).

There is, of course, much more to say and exciting topics to explore regarding the links between food and health. As well as discussions and debates[119] possible once one becomes aware of the multiple challenges it may involve, for humans, the environment, or for future generations.

---

[119] All the more so that studying human nutrition and diet in depth (and with a certain open-mindedness) leads to other fascinating questions, notably those related to evolution (or the interplay between studies on nutrition, understanding certain evolutionary facts, speculations about the lives of our distant ancestors, conclusions regarding our needs and our species, etc.).

Part 2: Survey on children's tastes, food representations, practices and education

Chapter 3: Presentation and behind-the-scenes of the survey

Before shedding light on the survey results, I propose to present the behind-the-scenes of it. In research, the conclusions reached are conditioned by a set of methodological choices made beforehand, which need to be explained. Here is a summary of the path I followed to successfully conduct this work, which also aims to immerse you in some facets of the sociologist's activity.

Choice of population and sampling

The desired study of representations and dietary behaviors of children led me to a qualitative field survey: involving semi-structured interviews, observation sessions at school, and collective interviews with classes. The decision to conduct semi-structured interviews required investigating children who were old enough, with sufficiently developed cognitive abilities to provide detailed responses, but also capable of overcoming shyness and remaining attentive and focused during interviews (which conventionally last about an hour in sociology).

After some tests during exploratory interviews, I realized that it was wise to focus on children aged at least nine years old. **The survey was eventually conducted with children aged nine to eleven, all enrolled in CM1 and CM2 classes (equivalent to 4th and 5th grade).** I focused on children (rather than adolescents and adults), both out of necessity[120] and because it seems to present some theoretical and practical advantages.

Indeed, **children are much more reliable than their parents when obtaining information about the food education they receive, as well as the diet of their parents** ("the truth comes out of children's mouth," as the popular saying goes). Some exploratory interviews with parents of students allowed me to understand that these were counterproductive actions: parents, when asked about their diet and that of their children, tend to quickly adopt a defensive posture, wanting above all to convey an image of "good parents" (which does not allow for the collection of relevant and reflective discourses).

The choice of elementary schools as the survey field has two main advantages for this research. Firstly, **it helped me to be able to interview children from diverse social backgrounds, thus aiming to obtain what is called in sociology a "representative sample" of the targeted "parent population" (French children).** Indeed, a qualitative survey allows collecting rich "data" (or narratives, when conducted through interviews) from a sample that aims to be representative of the entire population concerned by the research topic. In other words, if my work focuses on French children, I must select a (quantitatively restricted[121]) panel of children to interview

---

[120] As a doctoral thesis is supposed to be completed in three years, it is essential to make strategic and relevant choices regarding the population under investigation (in the case of sociology) and then narrow it down so that the research remains feasible in terms of time, budget, and energy.

[121] In a quantitative survey, for example, questionnaires will be distributed to a significant number of individuals (selected to form a sample): let's imagine around 3,000 people in a survey involving a single researcher. Subsequently, the brief and concise responses of the individuals who completed the questionnaire will be analyzed, cross-referencing them with variables (such as age, gender, socio-professional category) to achieve a quantitative sociology of the target population. Conversely, in the case of a qualitative survey, the focus will be on a limited number of individuals (around 30 to 50, for example, when a single researcher is involved), aiming to obtain a complex discourse from the respondents.

74

while ensuring that it can reflect the social reality of all French children.

While it would have been challenging to achieve such a representative sample outside of schools, they offered the opportunity not only to access the narratives of different children within the same institution but also to choose various types of schools, in which the profiles of children were diverse.

Secondly, access to school premises allowed investigating what was practiced in terms of food education. This part of the survey, however, remains somewhat limited, as it did not focus on specific institutions where particular food education actions were implemented but rather started with the idea of investigating food education practiced (or not) within schools chosen according to sociological sampling (with the randomness that implies).

I thus conducted a qualitative sociological survey in four elementary schools, involving forty children aged nine to eleven (semi-structured interviews), in eight CM1 and CM2 classes (collective interviews and experiments), as well as inside four school canteens (sociological observation sessions).

The schools, all located in Normandy, were selected according to three categories, as follows: two were in "priority neighborhoods of the city" in the Caen metropolitan area (hereafter referred to as "school A" and "school B"); one was in a small town with a median income higher than the national average ("school C"); and the fourth was a private, religious school presenting itself as specialized in nature education, located in the countryside ("school D").

Each of these three types of schools allowed me to access testimonies from children of very diverse social backgrounds (children of workers, executives, unemployed or jobless parents, immigrant parents or grandparents, teachers, self-employed individuals, artisans, tertiary sector employees, entrepreneurs, etc.). The children with whom I conducted interviews were selected by the teachers of the CM1 and CM2 classes of each school, attempting to involve children with different social profiles[122] and an equal number of boys and girls. Ten children were interviewed in each school.

In schools A and B, there were mainly children of factory workers, unemployed individuals, maintenance staff, or caretakers: what I will refer to as "disadvantaged social backgrounds. " School C was mostly composed of children from what we could call the middle class, with parents, for example, employed in the tertiary sector, artisans, secondary school teachers, a salon employee, bank employee, etc. I will refer to them as having "intermediate social backgrounds. School C also included some disadvantaged children. **School D mainly consisted of children from what I will term "affluent social backgrounds"[123] (parents were successful entrepreneurs, writers, self-employed individuals, restaurant owners), with some children from intermediate social backgrounds whose parents seemed to have a high cultural capital**.

Here is a table that summarizes the sample[124] of children who participated in the survey through semi-structured interviews, along

---

[122] Mainly based on their parents' professions, but also according to their foreign origins for the children of schools A and B, where they were predominantly children or grandchildren of immigrants.

[123] These designations have been formulated to provide a classification regarding the presumed chances of "success" (social and economic) for children based on their parents' situations, which are assumed to be linked to their income and assets. It is not a matter of aligning with a particular ideology or denouncing injustices, but rather observing notable differences in social origins among the interviewed children (differences sought for the sake of the survey, let's recall, in an attempt to obtain a representative sample of French children). Also, the term "affluent" is less precise than the other two, as it refers to parents' professions that still differ in terms of social status and income. I strongly doubt that there are many multimillionaires among the parents of the affluent» children interviewed. These are rather rural families whose situation is not uncomfortable, seeming to experience fewer financial constraints than «disadvantaged» or "intermediate" families. The rural aspect should also be considered as a sociological characteristic.

[124] One significant bias in terms of sample representativeness is that I did not interview children from affluent and urban social backgrounds. The affluent children I interviewed were grouped within School D, located in a rural area. It is

76

with their parents' professions and their school. I will note here that the names used are, of course, pseudonyms that I assigned to the children, and not their real names. These pseudonyms were chosen to reflect social reality as faithfully as possible[125].

Table No. 1: Nicknames of interviewed children and professions of their parents

---

highly likely that access to the perspectives of affluent urban children would have enriched the survey (for example, it is known that vegetarians are overrepresented among urban dwellers, yet I did not encounter any vegetarian children or those expressing having received a food education from their parents in that direction).

[125] But, of course, distant enough from them to ensure their anonymity. I chose to give false first names to children whose language is similar to that of their real first names, in order to take into account the foreign origins claimed by the children. This is obviously not about separatism but rather an attempt to faithfully present to the readers the profiles interviewed, especially since I noticed correlations between the claimed origin and certain preferences.

School	Nickname	Age	Father's occupation	Mother's occupation
A	Kasim	9	Unemployed	Unemployed
A	Anouar	9	Transporter	Nurse
A	Antoine	9	Unemployed	Unemployed
A	Yaprak	9	Site worker	Unemployed
A	Miriam	9	Site worker	Unemployed
A	Idriss	9	Unemployed	Housekeeper
A	Cindy	9	Market vendor (part-time)	Janitor
A	Paola	10	Deceased	Unemployed
A	Nelson	9	Compagny director	Nurse aide
A	Marvin	10	Absent father	Unemployed
B	Bilal	10	Factory worker	Unemployed
B	Martin	10	Unemployed	Unemployed
B	Boris	9	Building painter	Unemployed
B	Samba	9	Unemployed	Housekeeper
B	Khadija	10	Unemployed	Housekeeper
B	Mélanie	10	Mover	Unemployed
B	Yasmine	10	Factory worker	Unenmployed
B	Sonia	10	Security agent	Daycare worker
B	Yazid	10	Factory worker	Unenmployed
B	Hakim	9	Masonry worker	Janitor
C	Cassandra	10	Fireman	Skin consultant
C	Bastien	9	Cook	Estate agent
C	Marianne	10	Fishmonger	Clothing saleswoman
C	Kevin	9	Water technician	Baker
C	Lana	10	Bank worker	High school teacher
C	Gwenaëlle	10	Electrician (Self-employed)	Unemployed
C	Chloé	11	Enginner	Unemployed
C	Théo	9	Electrician (in a company)	Hotel receptionist
C	Amélie	10	Absent father	Secretary
C	Maxime	11	Carpenter	Unemployed
D	Apolline	10	Magazine editor-in-chief	Unemployed
D	Matteo	10	Site manager	School director
D	Octave	9	Owner of a fish company	Unemployed

D	Benjamin	9	Engineer	Bakery owner
D	Marius	9	Crane operator	Secretary
D	Corentin	9	Newspaper editor	Consultant
D	Samantha	9	Site manager	School director
D	Julie	9	Restaurant owner	City clerk
D	Kahil	10	Absent father	Housekeeper
D	Jonathan	10	Architect	Unemployed

I interviewed these forty children in semi-structured interviews, each lasting about an hour. I asked them questions about their food tastes and preferences, their representations of food pleasure, their daily habits (breakfast, lunch, snacks, dinner), the tastes and habits of their parents and in their families, their understanding of what "eating well" means, what their parents taught them about food, the food education they received at school, their representations of health, and the health education they received at school.

My approach to Sociology

I will briefly outline my conception of sociology, not in an objective and absolute manner, but from my perspective, which notably enabled me to conduct this research. It is true that we tend to see this term written and mentioned everywhere (media, news, political debates) without it always being clear to understand what it corresponds to.

There are many considerations about what sociology is, perhaps as many as there are sociologists or "schools" of thought. For example, making a so-called "critical" description of society by analyzing underlying power dynamics, a reflection primarily based on Marxist theory of "capitalism" (in the manner of thinkers from the Frankfurt School) or "modernity," or a study conducted by a private firm for a company on how to optimize its organization (and ultimately its productivity) are completely different activities, yet all can legitimately claim to be called sociology.

In other words, sociology is not a uniform discipline, as if there were only one protocolized and intellectual approach that allows studying everything. It is always good to be aware of this when exploring sociological works, which may also have the advantage of avoiding the pitfall and shortcut of making statements like "according to THE sociology, [I will refrain from providing examples here]."[126]

Sociology is a human science that involves the study, understanding, and description of everything related to the "social," i.e., everything that contributes to uniting or separating individuals from each other, both as individuals and as members of groups. **This includes behaviors and practices as well as everything in the realm of representations** (norms, symbols, cultures, customs, perceptions that differ depending on one's groups of belonging or origin, etc.). **It is akin to a science for at least three reasons.**

Firstly, because **its task is to understand reality as it is, not as one would like it to be**. And although it resorts to theory (or theoretical paths) to achieve this, **its goal must be to aim for the understanding of social reality as truthfully as possible**. In other words, **theory must always serve as a means to understand social reality, as an end**. If theory becomes an end in itself and not a means, sociology can no longer be a science but becomes itself a means, for example, to defend a cause.

Secondly, because **its practice requires methodological rigor or a strict research protocol to follow** (also called methodology), so as to optimize the veracity of its results or what is found through research. In this way, **observing people on the street or in the local café and then deducing big ideas about what "society" is or how it is doing is not sociology!** Methodological rigor involves making precise choices during all stages of research (initial theoretical and

---

[126] While this is more or less applicable to all academic disciplines and sciences, in the sense that a statement must always be understood within the context in which it was produced (epistemology, methodology, potential biases, limits, etc.).

contextual study, formulation of a problem and a research subject, selection of a population, definition of a field to investigate and its sample, development of tools adapted to this field for data production, data analysis, etc.), which can then be justifiable and defensible.

Thirdly, and in connection with the last points discussed, because it precisely requires the production of data or an "experiment" (what is called the empirical part of research), so that sociological theories do not come out of thin air. A theory or an idea must be based on real materials so that a research field can be compared to a laboratory.

It is commonly accepted that sociology is concerned with what is "socially constructed,"[127] meaning that what belongs to social reality is to be distinguished, even opposed, to everything that belongs to the "biological" or what is innate. **The uniqueness of my approach – that is, studying food representations and practices (assumed to depend heavily on a social dimension) while claiming to be "aware of the links between food and health" (not dependent on a social dimension) – involves focusing on what is socially constructed while being aware that this is not the case for all of reality**.

This idea may seem too obvious to need to be expressed but remains somewhat controversial, as it can carry a certain critical look at sociology itself. In other words, this proposes that **"just because the sociologist has been trained to be interested in what is socially constructed does not mean that he must conceive the entire reality as socially constructed." This stance requires a practice of sociology that includes an open mind and careful consideration of other sciences. It requires not engaging in a "war" between social sciences and "hard sciences" regarding whether this or that thing is "constructed" (acquired) or depends on certain**

---

[127] We could define what is socially constructed as that which varies across space and time (such as culture, norms, customs, or even ways of eating).

natural laws (innate). An interest in philosophy and dialectics will lead us to nuance rather than black and white.

Why an inductive approach?

It is essential, when engaging in research, to consider its epistemology. **Epistemology examines the ways knowledge is produced, addressing how, apart from the strictly methodological aspects, ideas in science are formulated**. This is fundamental because the conclusions reached in research, even if aimed at understanding reality[128], depend, at least in part, on their modes of production and thus their epistemology.

The ideas I will present here are sometimes technical and complex, so **I invite readers not interested in these issues to proceed directly to the next section**[129].

In sociology, as well as in research more generally, there is a tendency to distinguish deductive (or more precisely, hypothetico-deductive) and inductive (or empirico-inductive) approaches[130].

In the case of sociological research, the hypothetico-deductive approach involves formulating hypotheses—based on a sociological

---

[128] I start from the assumption that there is a (objective) reality that is independent of human perceptions (subjective) and that it is this reality that science aims to investigate (while being aware of all cognitive limitations that restrict us in achieving this).

[129] I have here attempted to make complex and specialized questions as accessible as possible. However, I am well aware that it may not interest everyone.

[130] In addition, see our article: Fardet A., Lebredonchel L., Rock E. (2021). Empirico-inductive and/or hypothetico-deductive methods in food science and nutrition research: which one to favor for better global health?. *Critical Reviews in Food Science and Nutrition*, Taylor & Francis, 2021, p. 1-14. https://doi.org/10.1080/10408398.2021.1976101

theory or a paradigm[131]—that will then be confirmed or refuted through field investigation, or the analysis of data not produced by oneself. For example, if we study the academic orientation of middle school third-year students and, based on Pierre Bourdieu's theory of reproduction (which posits that the French school system contributes to social reproduction, meaning it is likely that children of workers will become workers themselves, and the same for children of executives[132]), we formulate the hypothesis that "public schools encourage and prompt middle school third-year students who are children of workers to lean towards technical tracks, more due to a set of discriminations related to their social origins than based on their skills and academic level." We will then verify this through field research in schools[133].

This approach is relevant when the research subject is similar to the one in which theories are produced to formulate hypotheses. For Instance, studying the academic orientation of equivalent to ninth grade students based on Pierre Bourdieu's theories seems appropriate. It is indeed wise to refer to knowledge related to a similar subject and use it to approach research. This is actually a principle in science (established since Aristotle): one never starts from scratch and always begins by considering what has already been done in the same field.

This approach is conventional in the world of academic sociology (although it is somewhat implicit). It is customary not only to approach a research subject from a specific theoretical angle but

---

[131] That is to say, a set of representations and ideas that correspond to a comprehensive and coherent vision of reality, often giving rise to "schools of thought".

[132] Bourdieu P., Passeron J-C. (1970). *La Reproduction. Éléments pour une théorie du système d'enseignement*. Paris, Les Éditions de minuit.

[133] The inspiration of the moment led me to this example rather than another (also because I have supervised several similar works, where the topic was chosen by students, as a university instructor in survey methods, but mainly because it is simple to articulate and understand).

also, more generally, to have an affiliation, as a sociologist, with a school of thought or a certain paradigm. This is not without representing **significant potential cognitive biases**, with possible consequences being that these intellectual affiliations may, when working on a specific subject, lead to understanding it according to theories that were produced from a completely different research subject.

This is a somewhat complex reasoning, requiring me to provide an example again. Let's imagine that I work on the academic orientation of middle school third-year students and, feeling intellectually aligned with a Marxist paradigm, I decide to formulate hypotheses (which will guide the course of my field research) based on historical materialism[134], thereby confusing and mixing the idea of domination by means of production and the academic orientation of ninth grade students.

Although this could be interesting in substance, **there is a significant risk that I formulate theories or ideas that stem more from my ideological affiliation[135] with Marxism than aiding in the understanding of reality as it is** (regarding the academic orientation of ninth grade students). According to sociologists and epistemologists Barney G. Glaser and Anselm Strauss, **such a research endeavor would result in creating theories that are "not grounded,"**[136] meaning they are not in line with the social reality of the subject of interest.

In a critical stance towards deductive conventions in sociology (already in the mid-20th century), these two American sociologists

---

[134] Or, simply and vulgarly summarized, the Marxist idea (formulated by Marx) that what conditions history corresponds to the class struggles between the dominated (those who do not own the means of production) and the dominants (those who own the means of production)

[135] Glaser B.G., Strauss A.L. (1967). *The discovery of the grounded theory*. Chicago, Aldine.

[136] *Ibid*.

84

proposed to develop a set of foundations for an alternative epistemology in sociology, based on an inductive approach. It is also commonly referred to as the "grounded theory". **According to Glaser and Strauss: grounded theory can help to prevent the opportunistic use of theories that poorly match the data and whose explanatory power is doubtful.**[137]

This posture implies distancing oneself from the conventional deductive sociology, particularly with the aim of getting as close as possible to a neutral understanding of reality. **It often happens that a sociologist "develops a theory that embodies, without realizing it, their own ideals, the values of their profession and social class, as well as the representations and myths present in the population [...]. Such intended or unintended strategies lead to theories so detached from local daily realities that we don't really know how to apply them."**[138]

To avoid such biases, the grounded theory approach, and more generally, the inductive approach in sociology, involves conducting field research without "placing" oneself, prior to it, within a specific school of thought or paradigm, nor formulating a hypothesis based on an existing theory.

In other words, **it involves developing methodological tools that allow us to produce data without a theoretical bias regarding the reality concerning the subject of study.** This requires both efforts and a certain honesty in attempting to be as neutral as possible. It is also necessary to set aside one's views on the subject, at least during the time of the investigation and data analysis[139].

---

[137] *Ibid.*

[138] *Ibid.*

[139] A common criticism of the inductive approach in research revolves around the idea that "pure inductivism does not exist," given that the researcher remains an individual inevitably holding positions (and ideologies) specific to them (based on their background, influences, surroundings, etc.). This is, of course, not untrue in itself. The inductive approach, in a certain way, relies on the researcher's sincerity

Similarly, **it requires a substantial background of sociological knowledge**: since the goal is to develop a new sociology of a research subject, a sociologist adopting an inductive approach must have significant skills and knowledge. In other words, just because one is engaged in inductive reasoning does not mean one can do without theoretical knowledge.

In fact, these arguments in favor of the inductive approach and in critique of the hypothetico-deductive do not imply that one is superior to the other. Both simply have different uses, adapted to different situations and needs, depending on the nature of the research being conducted.

Once again, these somewhat lengthy and tedious epistemological explanations have likely revealed that **I adopted an inductive approach in the investigation I am about to present**. Firstly, because I wanted to approach the reality of the field as neutrally as possible, without the prior influence of any theory and paradigm. Secondly, despite the significant literature in the sociology of food (which is, of course, not ignored in my work), both French and international, I judged that the originality of my approach[140] deserved a fresh perspective, and it would have not been well adapted to existing sociological theories regarding nutrition[141].

What specifically did I investigate and how?

The investigation primarily relied on conducting semi-structured interviews with children, and I will quickly explain how they were

---

in this regard (the intention to be as neutral as possible) as well as an awareness of the limits in achieving such a pure neutrality.

[140] To study the representations and practices of food while taking into account their potential effects on health. This, at least to my knowledge, has not (or has been minimally) explored.

[141] Several sociological studies that have been conducted on children's nutrition and food education (both parental and at school) fall within a Bourdieusian paradigm. I will not fail to revisit some of them after presenting the survey results.

prepared and conducted. Here again, less curious readers may skip these explanations (though it is still essential to include them).

In qualitative sociology, interviews are used to gather the narratives of the individuals interviewed, providing access to a wealth of information and their representations[142]. **They are made effective through the prior preparation of an interview guide**, consisting of categories with systematically formulated open-ended questions. These questions aim for optimal and maximal openness in the discourse until reaching saturation of the information needed to thoroughly understand the reality of the subject.

The guide, always in view during interviews, also helps ensure that the same questions are posed to all those interviewed. This is absolutely essential; otherwise, a coherent comparative analysis could not be conducted.

"Continuous comparative analysis"[143] is the method that allowed me to analyze the narratives of the interviewed children and transform them into results. It involves **comparing the responses**, transcribed verbatim from audio recordings made during the interviews, of individuals asked the same questions, **analyzing the similarities and differences among them**. These differences and similarities in discourse gradually lead to the emergence of categories or groups (where a category gathers similar narratives across individuals, different from those similar to another group).

This process leads to the development of a typology of the studied population, or in other words, defining groups and attempting to understand the reasons for their existence. Theories will then offer interpretations as to why these groups exist. This is roughly what

---

[142] I will refer to the definition of the term representation proposed by Denise Jodelet in "*Les représentations* sociales" (traduced from French): that is, as "a form of knowledge, socially elaborated and shared, with a practical purpose and contributing to the construction of a reality common to a social group."

[143] Glaser B.G., Strauss A.L. (1967). *The discovery of the grounded theory. op.cit.*

qualitative sociology consists of[144], especially when conducted through interviews.

The interview guide was constructed with categories of questions formulated to saturate the children's narratives about their representations of food, practices, and their education about food (both parental and at school). In total, there were 8 categories of questions established, covering:

1) **Food preferences**: What do children like and dislike eating? (Encouraging them to provide as many examples as possible, often with follow-up questions); What brings them pleasure[145] in eating? (For example, on special occasions or holidays, or when they want to treat themselves?); What would children like to eat but cannot? (Due to parental restrictions or prohibitions).

2) **Practices, habits, and consumption**: Here, I asked children to describe their breakfasts, lunches at home and at school, dinners, snacks, and what they eat between meals. For each time of the day, I asked them to provide several examples, such as what they ate each day of the week or during the previous week, etc. I then asked a series of questions about consumption, i.e., food purchases and grocery shopping. (Who does the shopping in your family? When do you go? Where do you go? What do you buy? Why? etc.). These questions also provide interesting information about the child's family while transitioning to the next category.

3) **Food preferences and family eating**: This aimed to get an overview of the tastes and eating practices of the members of the child's family (what they like, dislike, eat often, etc.). It also aimed to find out how meals happen at home, with whom the child usually

---

[144] This is, of course, a simplified explanation, attempting to get to the essentials and be straightforward, according to my perspective.

[145] Several of these points, including this one, have been decided in part based on elements found in the literature (in sociology of food and other fields). I will refrain from justifying and explaining these details by citing the appropriate references here, mainly to avoid further complicating my argument.

eats, table manners, kitchen routines, who cooks, what the child can cook and has prepared before. Similarly, I asked the child about what their parents want them to eat or ask them to eat.

4) **Friends and their food preferences**: This set of questions was formulated mainly based on literature, but the questions posed did not yield relevant results to analyze. Nevertheless, I continued to ask these questions for practical reasons: after about twenty minutes, a seated child begins to tire of answering questions posed by an adult about things that do not always interest them. Giving children a few minutes to express themselves more freely and "talk about their friends," and then about their friends' food preferences, often revitalized the interviews, or in a way, gave the children a bit more energy. This kind of trick is also part of the sociologist's skill set.

5) **Health representations**: This was a rather delicate category to address and place in the interview guide[146]. It seemed important to obtain information about the health representations of the children in my research. However, asking health-related questions after asking about food might suggest to the respondents that I expect them to link the two and talk about their health representations in relation to food. Conversely, asking health questions before asking about food would probably have even more strongly influenced the nature of responses regarding food. So, I chose to approach this theme after questions about "friends," which somewhat allowed a break in the interviews and prevented a sudden transition from food to health. I asked what "health" means to the children, what it means to be healthy or unhealthy, how one stays healthy, what good lifestyle habits are, what illnesses the children know about, and if they have had close ones in poor health.

6) **Health education**: Exploring food and food education, taking into account the links between food and health, also required looking

---

[146] An interview guide should also be optimized to minimize potential biases related to the responses of the interviewees. The sociologist must ensure that they do not influence the discourse, or as little as possible.

into health education: what children have learned about health at school, what their parents have told them, and what advice adults have given them regarding health.

7) Knowledge of food and its links to health: I now return to food. The questions remain as neutral as possible, and the theme of the "links between food and health" is never explicitly mentioned to the children. I asked them what it means to eat well, what makes a good meal and a good food, and conversely, what it means to eat poorly, what makes a bad meal or bad food, and how they recognize them.

8) Food education: The questions asked are simple, asking children what their parents have taught them about food, what they have learned at school, and what they think about it.

These 8 themes were preceded by an introductory category: first asking children to introduce themselves, serving to obtain all the necessary information for any sociological investigation (age, parents' professions, place of residence, etc.). The start of the interviews was also the time to gain the children's trust and reassure them, emphasizing that their first names would not be disclosed, and they could say whatever they wanted ("your parents and the teacher won't know a word!").

The interviews took place during school hours; that is, while the children were in class, the teachers entrusted me with the children one by one. This had the advantage of giving a recreational form to our exchanges, taking the students somewhat out of their daily routine and offering them an extracurricular activity: they were all very happy to be chosen to participate (and also to miss an hour of class, in the process).

The situation would likely have been less beneficial to me, and the interviews much less fruitful, if they had taken place, as some academic inspectors wished, outside school hours. With introductions made and anonymity guaranteed, I discreetly tried to place the recorder on a corner of the table around which we were

90

sitting (usually without success, as such devices strongly piqued the interest of the children). And we were off!

Preamble to results and warnings

With forty children interviewed on these eight themes and all corresponding questions, the narratives I collected during this investigation are extremely rich. Children are indeed recognized as reliable and effective informants regarding what influences their eating practices, tastes[147], and the food education they receive from their parents[148].

In the following chapters, I will present the results that I find most interesting and relevant.

You will notice that most of them lead to categorizing the representations and eating practices of children based on their social backgrounds. In this regard, I have already received comments suggesting that this constitutes a bias, as I attempted to obtain a representative sample of French children based on social criteria with three categories of schools, and the categories of children constructed from the results are very similar to those defined to create the sample.

Simply put, this criticism assumes that I would have somewhat "forced" the results to fit categories established not after but even before the field survey. This is not the case. **The categories of children from "disadvantaged," "intermediate," and "affluent" social backgrounds emerged as results after my analyses, not**

---

[147] Waddingham S., Shaw K., Van Dam P., Bettiol S. (2017). What motivates their food choice? Children are key informants. *Appetite*, 120, 514-522. https://doi.org/10.1016/j.appet.2017.09.029 ; Scaglioni S., De Cosmi V., Ciappolino V., Parazzini F., Brambilla P., Agostoni C. (2018). Factors Influencing Children's Eating Behaviours. *Nutrients*, 10(6), 706. https://doi.org/10.3390/nu10060706

[148] Savage J.S., Fisher J.O, Birch L.L. (2007). Parental influence on eating behavior: conception to adolescence. *The Journal of Law, Medicine & Ethics*, 35(1), 22-34. https://doi.org/10.1111/j.1748-720X.2007.00111.x

before! I indeed sampled from ideal-typical (or caricatural) school categories to aim for the participation of children from various social backgrounds, but this did not influence the fact that their narratives later allowed me to observe that their representations and eating practices differ widely based on their social backgrounds.

As cliché as it may sound, it is factual: the "rich" do not have the same concepts and food consumption as the "poor," just as wealthy parents do not have the same strategies and approaches to food education as poor parents.

In his popular book "Rich Dad Poor Dad," Robert Kiyosaki presented the major differences between the relationship to money and its management that rich and poor parents have: so that the former have perspectives on what money is and strategies for its use that make them richer, while the latter lack these strategies and notions and consequently face a high probability of remaining poor. Although this book was not written based on a survey, it offers a narrative that seems to accurately depict reality.

My research allows me to understand that, similarly to what Kiyosaki described about money, affluent parents have conceptions of food and employ food education strategies that stand a good chance of contributing to their children's long-term health[149], while poor parents have representations and practices regarding food that will reinforce the likelihood that their children will be in poor health.

Of course, every time I assert that the tastes and practices of poor children are likely to contribute to making them sick, while those of affluent children are more likely to contribute to keeping them healthy, **it will in no way be about making a statement like "the poor: bad; the rich: good."**

---

[149] It's also not about taking a shortcut like "a healthy diet is enough for good health."

I think, however, that it is important to face the facts. Also, I do not think that staying in a relativistic discourse stating that "everyone has their practices and all this has no other consequence than social implications" - while simultaneously noting that health social inequalities continue to grow and the poorest are the most obese and suffer from chronic diseases - will allow us to make progress[150].

---

[150] To want to make progress here corresponds to the wish that the poor can at least have the means (and I am not specifically referring to financial means) to be less chronically ill (not less than the wealthy, but that they are already), in part thanks to nutrition.

Chapter 4: Disparities in children's tastes

Differences in the size of food repertoires

The first thing I observed when analyzing the children's responses regarding what they like and dislike to eat is that, despite sometimes persistent prompting, **those from disadvantaged social backgrounds consistently mentioned fewer foods and dishes than others**. This appears as a trend, so that **the more children were from poor families, the shorter and briefer the lists of foods they provided**. It was not a matter of shyness or children appearing particularly reserved, but rather what seems like a correlation between the size of food repertoires and the parents' professions.

Disadvantaged children generally cited fewer than eight foods or dishes they claimed to like or dislike. Those from intermediate social backgrounds tended to mention at least eight foods or dishes, while **affluent children typically listed more, often providing explanations about what they like and dislike and justifying their choices based on the health effects or certain properties of these foods**.

As an example, we can compare the responses of three children. Kasim, nine years old, whose both parents are unemployed, mainly stated liking "*kebabs and pizzas*." When I asked him to provide other examples, he hesitated for a moment, then confirmed that he liked kebabs and pizzas, and... that's it. I then asked him what kind of pizzas and kebabs he liked, what are they made of, and he replied that he likes "*all kinds of pizzas*," "*normal pizzas, you know*," and that he doesn't know what's inside.

To the same question, Cassandra, ten years old, whose mom is an esthetician (beauty salon employee) and whose stepfather is a firefighter, responded:

"Well, I like almost all vegetables except turnips and spinach, well, there are a few spinach that I like, Brussels sprouts too, I like them. Tomatoes and cucumbers, olives... Also, I like fries occasionally with chicken. Spaghetti Bolognese. I eat a lot of fruits, I love them. Well, except for apples, I love oranges, strawberries, bananas, clementines."

Julie, nine years old, whose mom is a notary and dad is the owner and operator of a restaurant, explained liking the "*good meat*" from animals owned by her parents or neighboring farms, which is consequently "*organic*," or "*kiwis because they have good vitamins in them [...] and they're tasty.*"

These are, of course, just examples, but they are not insignificant and accurately reflect the reality regarding the different styles of responses obtained.

It is also interesting to note that several affluent children have expressed what we could consider an indicator of a likely parental influence to maximize the size of their food repertoires or to emphasize its importance. This could, for example, be illustrated by a particular taste for "*fruits from other countries*" (such as passion fruit, kiwi, lychee, papaya), or other types of foreign or uncommon foods.

Differently constituted repertoires

You may have also noticed that these excerpts from responses vary not only in terms of the quantity of foods mentioned but also in the types of content. An important difference between poor children and others is that the former tend to talk about categories of foods rather than specific ones.

Many of them indeed stated not liking "vegetables" without providing many examples despite my prompts. Here, for example, is the response from Yazid, ten years old, whose dad works in a factory, and mom is unemployed:

"Vegetables! (Laughs) I don't like almost all vegetables... (I prompt him: like which ones?) Well, all vegetables, like cauliflower, that's horrible (he laughs). *I think the only one I like is the one in the tagine my mom makes sometimes, I think it's sweet potato."*

Despite the fact that other children (non-socially disadvantaged) mentioned vegetables as things they don't like, they always provided several specific examples of vegetables and never just referred to them as a category.

This was also the case regarding fruits, giving the impression that **disadvantaged children are less familiar with vegetables and fruits than others or have less to say about them.**

What came up more in their narratives, much more than in those of other children, was the mention of elements related to what we could call a register of foods, ingredients, and dishes commonly consumed in fast-food restaurants. This was observed in children whose parents work in precarious professions or are unemployed, both in schools A and B, as well as in school C. For example, Cindy, who primarily stated liking "hamburgers," "*McDonald's*," "pizzas, and tacos," also mentioned things she doesn't like, such as "ketchup," "samurai sauce," "Coca-Cola," or "Orangina."[151]

I often found this type of content in the responses of disadvantaged children, **while no child from intermediate or affluent social backgrounds mentioned such sauces or sodas.**

It is also possible to distinguish two subcategories of disadvantaged children concerning the foods and dishes mentioned as liked to be eaten. Those who do not have both parents from an immigrant background almost systematically affirmed, as their first response to the question, liking "hamburgers," "McDonald's," or "pizzas." Also mentioned by these children were "tacos," "sandwiches," and pasta. Those with both parents from an immigrant background (mainly

---

[151] When I questioned the children about their tastes, I also asked them what they like and dislike to drink.

from the Maghreb, sub-Saharan Africa, or Turkey) primarily cited "kebabs."

Among children with both parents from an immigrant background, the greatest diversity of foods in responses was provided by Nelson[152], whose father is a business owner; these were mainly Nigerian dishes, from his parents' home country.

In children from intermediate social backgrounds, "pasta" was also regularly mentioned as a liked food, accompanied by several vegetables and some fruits. The variety of examples provided being nothing like the responses of disadvantaged children.

A response that came up several times was "I like almost everything" or "I eat everything." When I asked what "everything" corresponds to, they generally replied with a list of several diverse and varied foods, as well as meat and vegetable-based dishes, or pasta and rice.

Some spoke of a few dishes found in fast-food type restaurants but in smaller quantities compared to the poorest children. It was often emphasized that it is important to consume this type of products "in moderation." Also, if vegetables were also among the least liked foods for these children, they were no longer mentioned only as a category but directly illustrated by diverse examples ("broccoli," "Brussels sprouts," and "beets" were most commonly mentioned).

Affluent children gave responses to these same questions quite similar to those of children from intermediate social backgrounds, generally a bit longer and more detailed, but with **two new elements that seem quite significant: homemade and organic.** These were commonly details following the mention of a food or

---

[152] Nelson appears to be from a rather affluent social background, at least based on the situation of his parents. However, his responses resembled those of both disadvantaged and affluent children, as he mentioned many elements related to fast food, while also citing several vegetables, fruits, meats, and dishes, explaining their effects on the body and health benefits.

dish, such as "*homemade bread*," "*organic oranges*," "*homemade soda* (or 'Coke')," or "*homemade hamburgers*."

Organic and homemade were associated with what they like to eat and what is good, and "chemical products" or "chemical" were associated by some affluent children with what they do not like. For example, Apolline explained not liking "McDonald's": "*I don't eat it because it's very chemical. There are lots of chemical products, in the minced meat, there's anti-vomit. Burger King is the same!*"

I thus distinguished three main categories of children based on their responses regarding what they like and dislike to eat. Disadvantaged children can also be differentiated into two subcategories, each with nuances: children with both parents[153] from an immigrant background and those without. Table No. 2 provides a summary of this categorization by capturing the main features of each of the specificities presented above.

---

[153] In several cases, when one of the two parents was not of immigrant origin, their responses were very similar to the children whose both parents are not of immigrant origin.

Table No. 2: Children's tastes

	What they say they like to eat	What they say they don't like to eat	Distinctive characteristics
Disadvantaged social origins; Both parents are from immigrant backgrounds	*Kebabs, pizzas, traditional dishes from their parents' country of origin*	"Vegetables" (often without specifying which ones); Many foods or dishes (or ingredients) found in fast-food restaurants (like "ketchup")	They generally mention fewer than eight liked and disliked foods or dishes; "Vegetables" are described as a category, with few or very few examples provided; Fruits are not mentioned (or are mentioned very rarely)
Disadvantaged social origins; Both parents are not from immigrant backgrounds	*Hamburgers, pizzas, pasta;* "*McDonald's,*" "*Burger King,*" *and other fast-food restaurant chai are often mentioned*		
Intermediate social origins	Diverse foods or dishes, including pasta, various vegetables, types of meat, and fruits	Diverse foods or dishes. Often includes vegetables such as broccoli, cabbage, and beets	They all mention more than eight liked and disliked foods or dishes
Affluent social origins			They justify their choices; Mention of "organic" and "homemade" as associated with the good, and "chemical" as associated with the bad.

Food pleasure

Children's responses to my questions about food pleasure are similar to those regarding tastes, in the sense that we can once again distinguish different types of content within them based on their social origins.

In fact, we find the same trends: the poorer the children, the more their representations of food pleasure seem to be linked to industrial and ultra-processed products or fast-food restaurants. This logically implies that, conversely, **the more affluent children are, the more their pleasure seems to be linked to artisanal or homemade foods**.

Those from disadvantaged social backgrounds often mentioned foods or ingredients found in fast-food restaurants (for example, "*ketchup*," "*samurai sauce*," "*Algerian sauce*," or "*barbecue sauce*"). Bilal, a ten-year-old whose father is a factory worker and mother is unemployed, responded: "*I really like cakes, like Prince chocolate*[154]. *Otherwise, what pleases me is sauces, ketchup goes with everything. The samurai sauce too, or the Algerian sauce in kebabs, mayo... or even all three mixed together.*"

Similarly, as observed earlier, **disadvantaged children did not provide much detail in their responses, often just mentioning categories** ("cakes," "candies"). For example, a girl seemed to particularly associate "*cheese pizzas*" with pleasure, without specifying which cheeses were involved. Here's an excerpt from her response: "*Uh... well, pizzas! Cheese pizzas! I could eat cheese pizzas every day, even all my life, I love pizzas too much.* (I ask again: pizzas with what kind of cheese?) *I don't know! All pizzas.* (I ask again: so broccoli pizzas too? (She previously mentioned hating vegetables, especially broccoli) *Oh no, not that!* (Laughs) (I ask again: is that all? What else?) *Yes, that's all! Pizzas!*"

---

[154] This is a popular industrial and ultra-processed biscuit in France.

The narratives of most disadvantaged children were very similar in this sense. Idriss, ten years old, whose mother is a janitor and father is unemployed, mentioned sandwiches and hamburgers as associated with his pleasure. When I asked him "sandwiches with what?" and "hamburgers with what?" he replied, "*I don't know, all hamburgers... Hamburgers with barbecue sauce inside.*"

Children from intermediate social backgrounds also often included foods or dishes found in fast-food restaurants. However, **these were accompanied by other foods or dishes that were not present in the responses of disadvantaged children** (including some savory items like "*chicken,*" "*mussels,*" "*lamb meat,*" "*raclette and raclette cheese,*" "*lasagna,*" "*minced steak with fries,*" or "*duck*").

In general, **associations between food pleasure and meat-containing dishes corresponded to meals consumed in fast-food restaurants for disadvantaged children, which was not the case for those from intermediate social backgrounds**. Moreover, the responses of the latter were more precise and detailed, including more examples of specific foods. Gwenaëlle, whose father owns an company as an electrician and mother is unemployed, stated that she finds pleasure in:

"*Custards, fries with minced steak or chicken, candies... iced tea, well, Ice tea. Also, hamburgers with fries.* (I ask again: you mentioned custards, what kind of custards? And hamburgers, what's inside?) *Oh yes, well especially custard when I said custard. For hamburgers, sometimes those from McDonald's, otherwise a hamburger with a homemade steak, gouda cheese, lettuce, and tomatoes*".

It seems that the food pleasure of children from intermediate social backgrounds is less associated with fast-food (although partially so) than that of disadvantaged children. It also includes more varied foods or dishes, more non-ultra-processed foods, and sometimes fruits or fruit juices.

The responses of affluent children follow what appears to be a trend: either containing even fewer references to fast food and industrial foods, more raw and whole foods, and even more precision, often accompanied by explanations and justifications. As an example, here is a quote from Apolline, ten years old, whose father is a magazine editor-in-chief and mother is unemployed:

"So, first of all, pancake parties! Pancakes and also raclettes, raclette cheese, tomme. I also really like Comté, you know, the cheese that doesn't smell very good. But that's only occasionally. Otherwise... vinegar! (She laughs) Well, when we put vinegar in dishes. Can we also mention drinks or not? Can we? So, orange juice, that really makes me happy! And especially when it's freshly squeezed from an orange. Also, Ice tea, but not often, or when we make it ourselves".

The mention of homemade food also frequently came up among socially affluent children when talking about their food pleasure, or the clarification that the pastries and cakes they like are *"made in a bakery."*

Table No. 3 summarizes the different characteristics that allow categorizing children's relationship to food pleasure, including some examples of sweet and savory foods mentioned.

Table No. 3: Representations of food pleasure

	Disadvantaged social origins	Intermediate social origins	Affluent social origins
Degree of industrialization and processing of food	Ultra-processed foods, fast-food restaurant chains, references to industrial food brands	Mentions of ultra-processed foods and fast-food chains, accompanied by more artisanal foods and dishes	Homemade, artisanal, raw foods, with occasional mentions of brands of industrial products
Examples of mentioned savory foods or dishes	*Kebabs, hamburgers, McDonald's,* frites, *KFC,* sauces de *fast-food*	*Hamburgers, McDonald's,* chicken, mussels, raclette	Cheeses, homemade crepes, avocados, chicken cooked with curry
Examples of mentioned sweet foods or dishes	Candies, industrial cakes, and biscuits associated with a brand	Candies, cakes, and bakery pastries	Squeezed orange juice, bakery or homemade cakes, homemade soda

These initial findings allow us to observe that children's tastes seem to vary widely depending on their social backgrounds. These contrasting tastes likely indicate practices and dietary habits that also vary according to these same parameters, with very different health effects.

Indeed, it appears that **the more children come from poor backgrounds, the more they seem to have internalized a set of tastes that may lead them towards practices favoring the development of chronic diseases**. What they like is associated with ingredients and industrial foods (often ultra-processed), indicating frequent visits to fast-food restaurants. Conversely, what they dislike often relates to vegetables, which they seem to be less familiar with.

In contrast, **the more children come from affluent backgrounds, the more they seem to have internalized a set of tastes that may lead them towards dietary practices that are more conducive to maintaining good health** (or at least less detrimental). For them, what is liked is associated with artisanal, "homemade,"[155] and "organic"[156] foods. Their tastes and repertoires are more varied and include more fruits, unprocessed animal products, and some vegetables, while what is disliked is often associated with industrial foods that they explain are not healthy.

The fact that these differences appear to be so marked pushes us to question the reasons for these contrasts. While there are theoretical elements and literature in the humanities and social sciences that can help elucidate this issue (which I will not fail to revisit), the upcoming responses from the children I will present also shed light on some theories and speculations on this matter.

What parents don't want their children to eat

The richness of the responses obtained (to the question "what would you like to eat but can't? For example, because your parents don't want you to?") allows for the outline of a sociology of eating restrictions imposed on children by their parents.

From the children's speeches, we understand that the social variations in tastes expressed by them are probably linked to styles of food education that also differ greatly according to the social positions of the parents.

It is known in family sociology that affluent parents tend to educate their children by using strategies to ensure they have a certain level of autonomy: corresponding to a rather "contemporary" mode of

---

[155] This does not seem unrelated to the desire to benefit from diet based on real foods.

[156] Which undoubtedly reflects an intention to try to avoid the ingestion of pathogenic chemical products.

education. While disadvantaged parents are more inclined to exercise authority, following a more "traditional" mode of education.

However, the opposite seems to be happening in the various parental food education strategies: so that the more parents are in affluent positions, the more they seem to impose restrictions and exercise significant regulation. Conversely, socially disadvantaged parents tend to allow more autonomy regarding their children's food choices, imposing fewer rules.

Based on the children's responses, it is possible to distinguish four types of restrictions and controls imposed on children by their parents.

The first is religious and was encountered in the responses of disadvantaged children and Muslim families. Several expressed undergoing controls on their diet by their parents, ensuring that it adheres to certain religious principles. For instance, Yazid, ten years old, whose father is a factory worker and mother is unemployed, declared:

"I like Napolitains, but I can't eat them because there is alcohol in them. Similarly, there's a cake I'd like to eat, I don't remember what it's called, but I can't because there's a bit of pork in it. Haribo candies, I've tasted them and like them, but later I found out there's pork in them, so my parents don't want me to eat them anymore."

It is interesting to note that these restrictions seem to have significantly contributed to shaping the conceptions of what "eating well" means among children from Muslim families. Later in the interviews, when I asked children to tell me what eating well means, several mentioned the idea that this is primarily related to religious respect, or, for example, that eating well is *"eating halal,"* or even *"eating with the right hand."*

Religious control over the children's diet is sometimes the only form of restrictions their parents impose (as Khadija, ten years old, whose mother is a janitor and father is unemployed, explained: "*I can eat whatever I want [...]. They tell me not to eat pork, and that's it. Oh yes, also we have to eat only halal meat.*")

The second type of restrictions and controls I found is related to parents' fear that their children will develop cavities or damage their teeth. It involves parents restricting the consumption of candies and sweets. This reality was expressed by several children from disadvantaged social backgrounds, but not by others.

The third involves limiting children's access to fast-food restaurants and the consumption of foods deemed "fatty" or "too salty" (or even "Coca-Cola," "McDonald's," "ice cream," and "hot dogs"), **with what appears to be a certain fear by parents that their children will become obese or "too fat."** This kind of restriction was only mentioned in the discourse of several children from intermediate social backgrounds. For example, Gwenaëlle said that she would like to eat more often at McDonald's: "*I would like to be able to go more often... Actually, I'm allowed for fries, but not ice cream and hamburgers, because it makes you fat. Well, it's fatty.*"

Children from intermediate social backgrounds often mentioned that they would like to eat more "hamburgers" or at fast-food chains, but their parents prevent them and try to limit their visits to once a week or every two weeks, or for special occasions.

The restrictions imposed by parents from intermediate social positions seem to be based on quantitative limitations of their children's food consumption. Several of these children also mentioned not being allowed to eat between meals (except for the snack, established as a real meal) and not being able to "feed themselves from the fridge" when they want, even if they say they are hungry.

The fourth type of restrictions and controls is related to what appears to be parents' fear of not knowing precisely what their children are ingesting, or more generally, a certain mistrust of industrial food, what comes from supermarkets, as well as

"chemical products" and the pathologies they can cause. This time, it is specific to parents from affluent social positions. Julie, nine years old, daughter of a notary and a restaurant owner, expressed that she would like to be able to drink Coca-Cola:

"I don't drink it often, sometimes for example I would like to, but my mother doesn't want me to because she says it will give me cancer. On the other hand, sometimes I drink a lot of lemonade... well, it's the same... often I'm not allowed, but well, I don't drink it every day. Then Fanta, well, it's the same, my mother doesn't want too, actually I'm not supposed to."

This somewhat corroborates my previous analyses regarding the association of several interviewed children from affluent social backgrounds between what they don't like (or what is bad) and foods that contain "chemical products." In addition to this example of *Coca-Cola*, other soda brands, (ultra-processed) breakfast cereals, as well as foods and dishes from large fast-food restaurant chains were also mentioned, access to which these parents prevent for their children.

It seems to be more about fears related to the quality of children's food consumption (rather than its quantity). Also, regulations and controls of food by affluent parents seem to be stricter and even more present in the daily lives of children.

Table No. 4 summarizes the different types of regulations and concerns regarding the effects of food on health that I found during the survey. Here again, we can arrive at a categorization of representations of nutrition (and the dependent modes of education), differing according to the social positions of the parents.

Table No. 4: Parental regulations and concerns regarding the effects of nutrition on health

	Disadvantaged social positions	Intermediate social positions	Affluent social positions
Awareness of the effects of food on health	Seems to be mostly focused on the fear of cavities	Manifests as fear of overweight and obesity, fear of what is "fatty," and being cautious about overeating at fast-food restaurants	Prevent consuming industrial products, eat as much organic and homemade as possible
Regulation of children's diet linked to health	Low (or absent): Mainly takes the form of warnings that sweets cause cavities	Medium: Eating fast food should remain occasional; Restrictions are more quantitative	High: Daily control and restrictions regarding the quality of food
Fears related to the effects of food on health	Fears that sweets cause cavities	Overeating (and too much "fatty" food) causes weight gain; Fears related to overweight	Fears of chemicals, or not knowing what is being ingested

I have also noticed that the only children who expressed having no dietary restrictions from their parents were all from disadvantaged backgrounds. This is the case with Antoine, nine years old, both parents unemployed, who stated, "*I can eat everything; my parents let me eat whatever I want,*" as well as Martin, ten years old, both parents unemployed as well: "*No, I can eat whatever I want. Sometimes I can even choose what I want to eat, for example, I can choose whether we go to Tacos, McDonald's, or Burger King.*"

These various fears and regulations by parents regarding their children's diet, in my opinion, reflect a certain correlation between social status and awareness of the effects of food on health (or, at least, different practices in food education that may indicate different levels of awareness). **It seems that the more parents belong to the "upper class" (or engage in activities that require significant education), the more they seem to have an awareness of the issues of nutrition in relation to health and employ suitable food education strategies.**

It appears that parents in precarious situations potentially have a limited awareness of the effects of food on health, as per the children's statements, focusing primarily on the fear of oral health problems[157]. Similarly, since, as we have seen before, obesity as a chronic disease constitutes a health problem, parents from intermediate social backgrounds, who seem to be particularly concerned, have what we could call an "average" awareness of these issues. The regulations of these parents seem to be primarily focused on quantitative limitations[158] of their children's food intake. As for parents from affluent social positions, they sometimes directly associate the risk of developing a chronic disease with industrial food products and seem to be concerned daily about what their children eat.

These levels of awareness lead to contrasting modes of food education, shaping children's tastes and habits differently, so that they have unequal backgrounds in dealing with the challenges of food for health.

---

[157] When one knows how quickly poor oral health can lead to high expenses, the concern of economically disadvantaged parents for their children's teeth is not incomprehensible (although chronic diseases also cost a lot, their financial impact tends to manifest more gradually and over the long term compared to dental care).

[158] I am trying here to understand what is at play in the representations of parents from intermediate social positions. The fact remains, however, that obesity is not only influenced by the quantity of what is ingested, but equally (or even more) by the quality (and also in the sense that lower quality, by disrupting satiety, often leads to a desire for a larger quantity).

Results consistent with other research on children's tastes and parental food education

I completely understand that such generalizing statements with significant societal and health implications, drawn from a qualitative sociological survey based on a panel of forty children, might raise doubts about their accuracy. It is not harmful, as a researcher, to be able to doubt one's own results and conclusions, especially when they seem as clear and straightforward as in the cases I have presented so far. The categorization of tastes, representations of children's nutrition, and different modes of education may also appear too simplistic to be true (to reflect reality, often complex, subtle, and nuanced).

In this sense, it becomes relevant to compare these results with those of other research conducted on similar subjects. The inductive approach, as I have described and presented previously, has the merit of ensuring that I was not influenced, before the survey, by observations made by other researchers[159]. Indeed, I discovered, entirely after formulating the analyses and conclusions I have reached here, that **the survey results are quite similar to those of other research on children's tastes and parental food education**.

Matching observations about socially marked differences in tastes have been made by Faustine Régnier and Ana Masullo. According to them, when individuals from affluent backgrounds are questioned about their tastes, they "immediately establish" a link between what they say they like to eat and health, while those from modest backgrounds "*claim to have a taste for things that are good because they taste good, not because they are good for health.*"[160]

---

[159] I have thus not been tempted to distort the reality of the field in a way that it could correspond to other observations made during research on similar subjects.

[160] Régnier F., Masullo A. (2009). Obésité, goûts et consommation : Intégration des normes d'alimentation et appartenance sociale. *Revue française de sociologie*, 50, 747-773. https://doi.org/10.3917/rfs.504.0747

In a study on different approaches to children's nutrition within school cafeterias, **Italian researcher Fillipo Oncini also observed that the more children come from affluent social backgrounds, the more extensive and varied their food repertoires are**[161]. According to him, **the main reason for this is that affluent parents are more invested in educating their children about food, imparting what he calls a "*differential advantage.*"**[162]

At home, their children are exposed to a wide variety of foods, including fruits and vegetables, as well as dishes presented as healthy. They also regularly go to restaurants, travel, and thus have the opportunity to taste world cuisines, contributing to the expansion of their repertoires. Conversely, **children from working-class backgrounds have less varied diets**. They often go out to eat with their families at pizzerias or fast-food restaurants near their homes. As a result, **they have less to say when questioned about their food consumption, while having limited ability to justify their food preferences based on health effects**.

According to Oncini, rich parents invest in food education (and its links to health) for their children in the same way they are more involved and attentive to help them with their schoolwork. This idea also aligns with the work of French sociologist Séverine Gojard, who observed that for affluent parents, feeding their child "*is part of an important educational process.*"[163]

It would indeed be strategies of food education that differ according to the social positions of parents. Several studies,

---

[161] Oncini, F. (2020). Cuisine, health and table manners: Food boundaries and forms of distinction among primary school children. *Sociology*, 54(3), 626-642. https://doi.org/10.1177/0038038519880087

[162] *Ibid*.

[163] Gojard S. (2000). L'alimentation dans la prime enfance, diffusion et réception des normes de puériculture. *Revue française de sociologie*, 41, 3, p. 475-512.

including those of Backett-Milburn et al.[164] and Fielding-Singh[165], agree that **the food education of affluent parents is stricter and allows less autonomy than that of precarious parents.**

The former provide less autonomy to their children regarding their consumption choices, trying to ensure that they learn to eat healthily and are able to internalize tastes they deem healthy. In contrast, poor parents, while not completely ignoring the links between food and health, are more flexible and grant more autonomy to their children.

This mode of education is explained by the fact that poor parents use nutrition as a "*means of combating deprivation*," or in other words, as a resource to prove to their children that they can satisfy their desires and thus be good parents, but also as a way to compensate for more expensive pleasures that are inaccessible to them[166].

This aligns with similar observations made by Régnier and Massulo, who found that industrial products and fast-food restaurants are valued in working-class environments as a form of compensation for other deprivations and because they represent "*evidence of participation in consumer society, from which members of modest categories are excluded by many other aspects.*"[167]

In working-class families, children and adolescents often try to avoid eating with their parents when they don't like their meals,

---

[164] Backett-Milburn K., Wills W., Roberts M.L., Lawton J. (2010). Food and family practices: teenagers, eating and domestic life in differing socio-economic circumstances. *Children's Geographies*, 8(3), 303-314. https://doi.org/10.1080/14733285.2010.494882

[165] Fielding-Singh P. (2017). A taste of inequality: Food's symbolic value across the socioeconomic spectrum. *Sociological Science*, 4, 424. https://doi.org/10.15195/v4.a17

[166] *Ibid*.

[167] Régnier F., Masullo A. (2009). Obésité, goûts et consommation : Intégration des normes d'alimentation et appartenance sociale. *op.cit.*

while affluent parents tend to insist that their children eat with them, without asking for their opinion on the meals they prepare[168]. When their children are picky eaters, **affluent parents constantly try to negotiate with them to find replacement foods that are considered as healthy as those refused**[169].

Middle-class parents find themselves somewhat caught between these two types of food education, aspiring to provide their children with the internalization of healthy representations and practices, while also trying to "compensate for their economic resources" with consumptions that would please them at the moment.

Another point that seems very interesting to me is that, according to Fielding-Singh's research, **the desires of socially disadvantaged children that their parents try to satisfy are very influenced by advertising and food marketing.** I will remind here that **food marketing specifically targeting children almost always corresponds to advertising campaigns for ultra-processed foods!**[170]

Advertising also reaches affluent children, who sometimes eat these products in secret, being forbidden by their parents. However, **parental control ensures that this consumption remains limited**. To illustrate this observation by Fielding-Singh, I could take the example of a child who mentioned that she occasionally eats industrial brand cakes and candies when she is looked after by her grandmother, and her parents are very upset if they find out.

---

[168] Backett-Milburn K., Wills W., Roberts M.L., Lawton J. (2010). Food and family practices: teenagers, eating and domestic life in differing socio-economic circumstances. *op.cit.*

[169] Fielding-Singh P. (2017). A taste of inequality: Food's symbolic value across the socioeconomic spectrum. *op.cit.*

[170] Mallarino C., and al. (2013). Advertising of ultra-processed foods and beverages: children as a vulnerable population. *op.cit.*; Martines, R M. et al. (2019). Association between watching TV whilst eating and children's consumption of ultraprocessed foods in United Kingdom. *op.cit.*

These few findings from empirical research and theoretical reflections by other researchers seem to entirely match my analyses and theories regarding different styles of education that vary according to the social positions of parents, greatly influencing the representations, knowledge, and apparently the tastes of their children regarding food.

These distinctly socially marked differences[171] **involve major challenges, probably including habits and practices whose effects on health would also be profoundly different** (if the practices were in line with the mentioned tastes and deduced food education types). This is what we will now try to verify by continuing the presentation of the survey results.

---

[171] Of which we now know that their reality is not limited to the sample of children interviewed during this survey, nor even to France.

Chapter 5: What children eat based on their social backgrounds, or the making of future social inequalities in health

I will remind you right away that the results I will present here do not come from direct observations of the meals and purchases of children and their parents but are based on the narratives of the children, which always carries a certain risk in terms of reliability. For example, if half of them were lying, the data would not be worth much. However, this is unlikely, also because **these narratives of what they are used to eating correspond to the reality that has gradually emerged from the analyses conducted so far, allowing, once again, the categorization of children's diets according to their social backgrounds.**

Breakfasts

Disadvantaged children have almost systematically mentioned ultra-processed *Nutella* spread, often as one of the main components of their breakfasts. In fact, the only ones not to have mentioned *Nutella* are three girls who said they don't eat anything in the morning. I write "spread," but the children all talked about "*Nutella*," with what appears to be an agreement on the brand's importance. The breakfast mentioned by Cindy, nine years old, attending school A, whose parents are the building caretaker where she lives and a market vendor (part-time job), fairly reflects the breakfasts of most of these children:

"I drink milk, we often heat it in the microwave, and also Nutella. (I prompt her: and what else?) Just Nutella. (Prompt: Nutella, with nothing else?) (She laughs) Yes, yes! I love it too much; I just take Nutella, put the spoon in it, and eat it like that while drinking my milk. (Prompt: every morning?) Not always, other times I just drink warm milk; if I'm not hungry, I don't take Nutella; otherwise, I take it, or if I'm really hungry, I take a bit of bread and dip it in Nutella."

Nutella **is often accompanied by a piece of bread or an ultra-processed biscuit** (brands that are popular in France were mentioned), **as well as a bowl or glass of milk, or less frequently, a glass of fruit juice**. The compositions of breakfasts for disadvantaged children are very similar in this sense. As a comparison with Cindy, Bilal recounted:

"Every morning, well, I take a bowl, put milk, put chocolate, and mix it; then, I take the bread specially baked in the oven; it's nice and warm. I remove the bread crust and put a lot of Nutella, then I dip it in milk. Sometimes, my parents help me prepare it, but sometimes it's me, and I eat that every morning."

Others, in the minority, mentioned *"cereals with milk"* (ultra-processed cereals marketed for children), or **certain soda brands**. It seems relevant to note that the two disadvantaged children from school C described breakfasts very similar to those from schools A and B, while Nelson, the only socially affluent child attending school in a priority district of the city, spoke of different compositions.

Breakfasts for children of intermediate social backgrounds are mostly composed of a bowl of milk with "cereals" (always ultra-processed products marketed for children) **or a glass of milk or fruit juice accompanied by a pastry** (chocolate bread or croissant), but **also one or two fruits** (apples, bananas, oranges, kiwis, clementines, blueberries, and cherries were mentioned). The breakfast of Lana, ten years old, whose mom is a teacher at the middle school, and dad is a bank employee, is a fairly representative example, consisting of *"white chocolate cereals with a bowl of milk,"* with *"at least two fruits every day, an apple and a clementine, or sometimes cherries."*

Those of affluent children are more varied and sometimes quite different from each other, so it is not relevant to propose a typical breakfast through a single narrative. We still find regular mentions of the words "organic" and "homemade." The responses are often longer and generally contain more foods per child than all the

combined responses of disadvantaged children. Apolline, for example, said:

"Well, I take slices of bread with jam, especially plum jam, organic. Sometimes, but not often, we eat cereals with wheat and chocolate. (Prompt: what kind of cereals are they?) It's a muesli mix with various cereals; I don't know exactly what's in it, but I know there are also raisins. When there's nothing left, actually, we take what's left when we have to do the shopping. Also, sometimes orange juice. After, this is rare, but sometimes we take yogurt, but not chocolate yogurt, only plain yogurt. We also take fruits, an orange or a banana, and... that's all for breakfast."

"Cereals" were also mentioned, but it was not the same type of products. Benjamin specified when I asked which cereals he was talking about: "***It's oat flakes and oat-based things, oat cereals. It's like the cereals we see in commercials, but here it's good for health.***" Other examples of foods consumed in the morning by these children include **eggs (organic was specified), bacon, toast with jam (homemade), but also fruits (at least two were mentioned by each child)**.

Here, we can establish a correlation between the social background of children and the health effects of their diet, incorporating all the criteria developed previously to conceive a healthy diet. In other words, according to the narratives I have collected in the field, **the more children come from disadvantaged social backgrounds, the less their breakfasts are composed of real foods, the less varied (and balanced[172]) their diet is, and the more they seem to ingest chemical products!** While the breakfasts of children from poor parents are mainly composed of ultra-processed foods, affluent children benefit from a rather whole foods based and varied diet, that tends to avoid the ingestion of chemical products.

---

[172] A breakfast consisting solely of ultra-processed carbohydrates and additives (such as industrial chocolate spread) cannot, even through various intellectual or marketing contortions, be considered balanced.

Additionally, in school D, fruits are offered to them in the morning before recess, even though they already consume almost all of them at home before school. **Such marked and significant differences could almost make sense in light of the observed growing social health inequalities mentioned earlier.**

Table No. 5 synthesizes the categorization of children based on what they have reported eating during their breakfasts:

Table No. 5: Children's breakfasts

	Disadvantaged social origins	Intermediate social origins	Affluent social origins
Consumed frequently	Glass or bowl of milk, piece of bread or ultra-processed biscuit, spread (*Nutella*)	Bowl of milk, glass of fruit juice, spread (*Nutella*), (ultra-processed) cereals for children, a piece of fruit	Organic or homemade bread and jam, two fruits, a yogurt, cereal mixes (for example, with oat flakes)
Consumed occasionally	Glass of fruit juice or soda, (ultra-processed) cereals for children	Two different fruits	In school D, children sometimes eat a fruit distributed at school in the morning

Lunches (outside the school canteen)

I will address here the responses of the children regarding their habits during lunchtime meals, excluding those taken at the school canteen. We can still distinguish three categories of children based on their lunches according to their social backgrounds, although two subcategories clearly emerge among the disadvantaged.

Lunches are indeed somewhat different depending on whether both parents are of immigrant origin or not. **Children from poor families with both parents of immigrant origin mostly seem to have lunch outside very regularly, mainly nourishing themselves with kebabs** and pizzas. **When they have lunch at home, which seems to happen infrequently during the week, they sometimes eat traditional dishes from their countries of origin**. It is interesting to note that **these dishes often contain several vegetables, but these children tend to try to avoid them**. The response of Anouar, nine years old, who introduced himself at the beginning of the interview as "Algerian," summarizes this reality well:

"*When my mother is tired, I eat kebabs or pizzas or tacos outside, or even when I go with my older brothers, but in fact, it's almost every day. Otherwise, sometimes I also eat at home for lunch, for example, on Mondays; sometimes I eat tajine, couscous, chicken with vegetables, but well, I don't like it.* (I prompt: what's in the couscous then?) *Well, in the couscous, my mother prepares the couscous, then she puts sauce, and then she puts vegetables, but only the ones I like because I don't like vegetables* (Prompt: what vegetables do you like then?) ***Well, I like zucchinis, and... what else? I don't know what it's called, but it's green, it's chili.*** (Prompt: and what's in the tajine?) **In the tajine, she doesn't put vegetables, she puts chicken, pasta, sweet and savory, and it's so good.**"

Disadvantaged children whose parents are not of immigrant origin, or of whom only one is, do not have the habit of eating out as much during their lunch meals. At home, the main products that make up their lunches are pasta, pizza, mashed potatoes, ham, sausages, or hamburgers. The examples given are quite similar among different children.

Sonia, whose both parents work and who eats at the canteen during the school period, explained that when she eats at home for lunch, on Wednesdays and during school holidays, **pasta, ham, and pizza are simple and quick dishes that children can warm up themselves in the microwave. Disadvantaged children commonly do not mention vegetables when describing their lunches. It is also quite common for them to eat meals purchased from fast-food restaurants at home**. When both parents are of immigrant origin, particularly from North Africa or Turkey, it is mainly "kebabs" and "pizzas," while for others, it's "McDonald's" and "pizzas."

Children of intermediate social backgrounds recount more varied lunches, generally including at least a dozen different foods and dishes given as examples. These include several vegetables and legumes, as well as various types of meats and fish. Here is an excerpt from a 10-year-old girl's response (before any prompting from me): "*Sardines, fries, beef meatballs, green beans, chicken, zucchini or potato gratin, grated carrots, beets. Also, spinach sometimes, or starchy foods, potatoes.*"

Affluent children had similar responses in terms of content, with, however, more frequent mentions of homemade items (like "*the bread that dad makes*"), **as well as explanations and justifications about what they eat, based on potential health effects**. For example, Corentin, nine years old, explained that "*onions are good for the throat and stomach*" and are included in most meals he eats at lunch.

Table No. 6: Children's lunches (outside the school canteen)

	Disadvantaged social origins - parents from an immigrant background	Disadvantaged social origins - parents not from an immigrant background	Intermediate social origins	Affluent social origins
Examples of frequently eaten lunch meals	*Kebabs*, pizzas, Traditional dishes from the parents' country of origin	Pasta, ham, sausage, *pizzas*, *McDonald's*	Various dishes and foods, mentions of various vegetables, starches, meats, fish, and legumes	
Distinctive features	The meals are not very varied, with few or no vegetables (although they are present in the dishes from the parents' countries of origin, they are often avoided). Kebabs are often eaten outside the home. Meals are described as "easy to prepare" and sometimes reheated by the children		The meals are varied, with at least two vegetables mentioned per child, as well as several types of meat and fish	The children justify and explain the effects of what they eat. Homemade food is mentioned

Some observations regarding meals eaten in the school canteen

The brief analysis I present here attempts to establish a connection between the semi-structured interviews conducted with children and the few observation sessions I carried out in the school canteens of schools A, B, C, and D.

School D must be considered separately because it does not include an usual canteen: children have lunch within the school in a dedicated room, eating what their parents have prepared and provided in transportable containers. During observation phases, these meals were quite diverse, and their examination does not seem to have as significant sociological interest as what has been discussed so far.

Upon obtaining permission to investigate in school B (located in a priority district of the city) negotiated with the education department of the municipality, I was tasked with submitting a report on food waste to them after my investigation. I learned that food waste, substantial in this school, was perceived as a real scourge by the officials. Some schools located in priority districts of the city may receive additional subsidies, thanks to which the school canteen of school B offers meals composed of organic and local foods several times a week. These mainly include organic and local vegetables and legumes, which, as you can imagine, come at a certain cost.

The walls of the canteen were, in accordance with measures taken by the municipality, adorned with large posters on which several slogans accompanied by drawings were inscribed, aiming to "fight against food waste."

These measures seem to be ineffective, both according to what I observed on the ground and according to the children's statements. Several of them explained to me that they do not like most of what is served in the canteen, except for fries, chicken, yogurt, couscous, or bread. As a result, **some children will sort through the foods that make up their meals, ultimately ending up eating only "the yogurt and a piece of bread"**. As seen earlier, most of these children[173] are not accustomed to consuming vegetables at home, and greater autonomy, in general, is allowed in terms of what they want to eat.

---

[173] Schools A and B, located in empoverished neighborhoods, are almost entirely attended by children from socially disadvantaged backgrounds.

It is not surprising that food waste is particularly significant in this type of school. Moreover, the sight of slogans does not seem to resonate much with the children, nor does it speak to them in any way. **They seem to assimilate them as directives without really giving them meaning: phrases like "finish your plate" ultimately appear quite similar to "clean your room" – orders given by adults that, if they cannot be forced or compelled to be executed, will not be carried out because it doesn't make sense to the children.**

During the school B canteen meals, supervisors regularly encourage children to taste everything served to them, often without success. In any case, taking a bite to taste does not mean that they will finish the dish. **It is quite astonishing that, aside from these slogans scattered throughout the canteen, the interviewed children from school B told me they had never discussed about food at school.** I will come back to this.

Some children of intermediate social backgrounds in school C also stated that they do not particularly like what is served in the canteen; however, food waste during meals at this school is lower. It is very likely that this is related to the fact that these children are used to varying their diet at home, especially by regularly eating vegetables. In general, children from school C seem to enjoy their canteen meals more than those from schools A and B, even though it does not offer organic or local foods. For example, Cassandra explained:

"At the canteen, almost every noon, we have a starter, we eat a lot of meat, we have meat almost every noon, and then it's starches or vegetables. (Prompt: for example?) pasta, potatoes, sometimes green beans or white beans, but more often starches. For dessert, we have chocolate éclairs and fruits, clementines." She did not express particular criticism regarding the meals served.

Here, I prefer to once again use caution and emphasize that I am not suggesting that disadvantaged children behave "poorly" with food, while wealthier children behave better.

It is rather to draw attention to the fact that complex problems of this kind cannot be solved with simple moralizing slogans, at least according to what emerges from the reality on the ground. Regardless, despite more expensive meals, including organic and local products served at school B, children from school C seem to have a more varied and balanced diet than those from school B. The same is true in school A, where portions of vegetables, salads, or legumes were rarely finished during observation sessions. The fact that I noticed this tendency of food waste in two schools located in priority districts of the city does not necessarily mean that this is generalizable as a reality specific to this type of school[174]. However, it is probable and logical that food waste, often resulting in an unvaried and unbalanced diet, is at least partly due to serving foods to children who are not accustomed to consuming them at home, without undertaking any real pedagogical action in parallel[175].

My analysis remains limited here, particularly because I did not investigate schools that implement specific and elaborate actions for food education that take place during canteen meals.

Afternoon snack

For all the children interviewed, afternoon snack appears as a real meal, a conventional moment during which children are allowed to eat outside the three main meals, especially sweet products. Again (which should no longer be surprising), snack compositions are markedly different based on the social backgrounds of the children.

Those who are disadvantaged mainly consume ultra-processed industrial biscuits (with the most mentioned brands being *Prince*,

---

[174] Outside the research context, I have personally had the opportunity to work temporarily within a school canteen of a school located in a priority neighborhood of the city, where the educational policy was much stricter than in schools A and B. The waste there was less.

[175] Yes, displaying posters with slogans is not a genuine educational action.

Oreo, Petit-beurre, Lu). They also, but less frequently, consume **candies** (for example, "*Haribo*," "*spicy candies*," or "*Dragibus*"), **as well as a glass of soda**[176]. Some of these children again eat **a piece of bread with "*Nutella*" spread**. One boy mentioned, among other things, having "*waffles dipped in Nutella every day at five o'clock,*" and a girl said she eats "*mostly candies, Smurfs or sour candies, or a piece of bread and Nutella.*"

Those from intermediate social backgrounds instead consume pastries or desserts for snacks, although some children, in the minority, also mentioned some ultra-processed biscuits. None of those interviewed mentioned candies. Their snacks also often consist of a glass of orange juice or another fruit juice, and sometimes a whole fruit (such as apples, clementines, oranges, pears, or bananas). Chloé, eleven years old, whose father is an engineer and mother is unemployed, described her snacks as usually containing:

"*A chocolate croissant from the bakery or a Pepito, which is a bit like a chocolate croissant but different, with orange juice or sometimes an orange.*" Similar to the discourse of a wealthy child mentioned earlier, Chloé also added: "*With my grandma, sometimes we eat a lot of chocolate when I have a snack at her place, cakes or even some candies, and my parents are a little upset if they know about it.*"

The recurrence of this type of narrative suggests that significant differences found between the contents of children's meals based on their social backgrounds are likely related to regulations imposed by parents, with more significant autonomy and choices left to poor children by parents and stricter control set by wealthier parents.

The snacks of wealthy children are similar to those of children from intermediate social backgrounds and differ little, except through mentions of homemade items, for bread and jam. Their snacks are

---

[176] You may have guessed it, the photograph on the book cover, which I took myself, is inspired by the snacks described by disadvantaged children (in an exaggerated version).

mainly composed of a pastry (chocolate croissant or croissant purchased at the bakery) or artisanal bread with jam (which here replaces the spread), and a glass of fruit juice (freshly squeezed) or a fruit. A "glass of organic milk" and "organic yogurt" were also mentioned by two children.

Table No. 7: Children's afternoon snacks

	Disadvantaged social origins	Intermediate social origins	Affluent social origins
Examples of foods frequently consumed	Ultra-processed biscuits, soda, *Nutella* spread, a piece of bread	Pastries, fruit juice, a fruit	Pastries, fruit juice, a fruit, jam, bread (homemade or organic)
Examples of foods consumed occasionally	Candies	Ultra-processed biscuits	Glass of milk or yogurt

Dinners

I will conclude this analysis of children's meals based on their testimonies by comparing the different types of dinners mentioned. Similar to the lunches outside the canteen, we can distinguish two subcategories among disadvantaged children, still depending on whether both parents are immigrants or not.

In the case of the first group, dinners alternate between dishes from their parents' countries of origin (for example, *tajine*, *chorba*, *harira*, or *chicken yassa*) and pizzas, tacos, or kebabs with fries, which are bought externally and eaten at home.

The second group frequently mentioned prepared dishes or those that correspond to what is consumed in fast-food restaurants ("*McDonald's*," "tacos," "pizzas," "hamburgers," "*Coca-cola*," and other sodas, etc.), as well as "noodles," "sausages," "mashed

potatoes," and "ham." For example, here are the responses of Martin, ten years old, whose both parents are unemployed, and Paola, ten years old, whose mother is a widowed unemployed:

"In the evening, we either have McDonald's or takeout. We order things like McDonald's, tacos, but most often McDonald's, or sometimes pasta"; *"Often, we eat if there's something left from the morning, well, from noon, well, we eat what's left. And if there's nothing left, we make something easy, like tacos, or pizza, or other easy things, hamburgers, we don't spend much time cooking.* (Prompt: you said 'we,' do you also cook?) *Yes, a little, everyone does something except my brother. For example, I prepare the pizza, I put it in the oven or microwave, my sister sets the table, and that's it"*.

We notice here that the expression of "time-saving" during the preparation of lunch and dinner frequently appears in the narratives of all these children: meals often need to be ready quickly and be easy to make, like pre-prepared dishes bought in supermarkets, pizzas, or burgers to reheat in the oven or microwave, etc.

The fact that both parents are immigrants or not includes some differences and nuances in the composition of children's meals but seems to be much less decisive than social position. This idea is supported by comparing the responses of Marvin and Nelson, two children whose parents are from Nigeria but have contrasting social positions.

Marvin, whose mother is unemployed, and the father is absent, said he eats *"the same thing as at noon, except we add KFC or McDonald's when my mom goes out, she brings it for us for the evening, she buys KFC or tacos or kebab."* Nelson, whose father is a business owner, said, however: *"At our place, in the evening, we eat rather balanced, vegetables with steak, rice, spinach, cucumber, green beans, Banga, salad, tomatoes, or broccoli, and... that's all, I think."*

Hamburgers, pizzas, and *"McDonald's"* were also mentioned by children from intermediate social backgrounds but as occasional

rather than daily consumption. They are more often replaced by "*croque-monsieur*" or homemade "hamburgers." Soup, broth[177], pasta, chicken, beef, green beans, carrots, or savory pies are among the dishes regularly mentioned. Some children mentioned occasionally eating pastries for dessert, a piece of chocolate cake, or fruit tart. The responses were always varied and consisted of a greater number of different foods and dishes than those of disadvantaged children. Bastien, nine years old, whose parents are a real estate agent and a restaurant chef, explained, for example:

"*We eat soup! Well, most often, but when there's none left... either it's crepes, sometimes it's pizza, or pasta and meat.* (Prompt: what's in the soup? What kind of meat is it? What's in the pizza?) *The soup, well, it's vegetable soup, but I don't always know what she puts in it... since my mom makes it, I just know there are often carrots. The meat, well... about the same as on Wednesdays, steak or chicken escalope. The pasta is often small pasta or butterfly pasta. Or the pasta that's full of cheese inside!*"

Marianne, ten years old, whose mother is a clothing store saleswoman and the father is a fishmonger, was the only child from intermediate social backgrounds to link her diet to beneficial effects on her health. She explained:

"*In the evening, I eat... soups, and what's it called... beef stew... but well, I eat more vegetables in the evening because it's better for health. For example, carrots with potatoes or beans.* (Prompt: why is it better for health?) *Because you digest better and faster when it's vegetables, whereas you don't digest well when it's... when it's too heavy, and it's better to go to sleep right after.*"

The dinners of affluent children unsurprisingly follow the same trends outlined so far. The dishes and foods most mentioned by them are soups, broths, vegetables (green beans, spinach,

---

[177] The majority of the field investigation was conducted during the winter (2018-2019).

broccoli, carrots, leeks, cucumbers), spaghetti bolognese, organic eggs, organic yogurt or from a farm, and a little less frequently, meat ("steak," "chicken," "beefsteak," or "sheep"). Organic and homemade items are still present in their narratives, perhaps slightly more than when they talked about their other meals.

Table No. 8: Children's dinners

	Disadvantaged social origins - parents from an immigrant background	Disadvantaged social origins - parents not from an immigrant background	Intermediate social origins	Affluent social origins
Examples of frequently eaten evening meals	Dishes from the parents' country of origin (*tajine, chorba, harira,* chicken *yassa, couscous*), pizzas, *kebabs, tacos*	Pasta, ham, mashed potatoes, pizzas, hamburgers (*McDonald's* is also frequently mentioned)	Varied dishes, often homemade soups and broths, different types of vegetables and meats, pasta, eggs, yogurt, savory pies	
Meal preparation	Pizzas and *kebabs* are often bought outside and eaten at home	The dishes are often pre-prepared for reheating in the microwave, easy and quick to prepare, or bought from outside	Some components of the meal are described as homemade (for example, soup or broth, pizzas, or croque-monsieur)	The components of the meal are mostly described as homemade, and some products are organic and/or locally sourced

Children's narratives about their parents' food purchases and tastes

I will try to be brief here, especially since the children's responses intended to provide information about their parents' food purchases do not bring much novelty or surprise compared to what has been presented so far.

Disadvantaged parents, often workers or unemployed, mostly do their shopping in hypermarkets and supermarkets close to their place of residence or sometimes in local butcher shops. **They also very often buy food for their children in fast-food restaurants, which are located next to or outside the hypermarkets they frequent.** Middle-class parents also do their shopping in supermarkets and hypermarkets, occasionally complementing them at local markets, grocery stores, bakeries, and butchers. Parents of the so-called "upper" class do some of their shopping in supermarkets, at the market, in butchers, but also in organic grocery stores, or sometimes directly on farms. They sometimes make long car trips to specialized outlets that meet their requirements.

Beyond these rather expected pieces of information, what seems more interesting in **the children's narratives here is that they confirm my analyses, as well as those of the research I have presented, regarding the fact that the wealthier the parents are[178], the more they impose strict control and regulation on their children's diet, based on its health effects.**

It also seems that, contrary to what one might think, children of poor parents more often accompany their parents for shopping. When parents are immigrants, it is common for little girls to help their parents speak and better understand French in stores. When the children of the poor join their parents, it is common for the

---

[178] Although education and cultural capital also seem to play a significant role, not just strictly social position or wealth.

parents to let the children choose a part of what they buy. Parents of intermediate and affluent social backgrounds do not let their children choose what to buy when it comes to products they consider bad for health. The following example, narrated by a child, illustrates this:

"My mom rarely wants me to go shopping with her because I often ask her anything and everything, especially candies [...], and then I get scolded, and anyway, she doesn't want to buy them. Every time I go with my mom, we end up with lots of fruit juices and fruits, instead of the candies I want. When we go shopping with my mom and stepfather, they don't like it because they don't want to buy just anything."

Wealthy parents, instead of simply forbidding their children from selecting certain products, try at the same time to make them aware of the harmful effects on health that their consumption would have, but also sometimes of certain reasons that tend to justify buying one product instead of another (for example, ecological reasons or animal welfare).

Regarding the tastes of parents according to their children, we find discourses that often follow the trends outlined so far. However, major differences have been observed between poor parents from immigration backgrounds and those who are not. In general, the former seem to like and consume more whole foods, most of the time eaten within dishes from their countries of origin: several vegetables have been regularly mentioned, as well as several types of meat. For example, Yazid said:

"My dad really likes vegetables and meat, well, when we eat couscous or tajine. My mom is a vegetarian; she doesn't eat any meat at all. She eats vegetables, soup, especially harira, and that's it. (Prompt: so what meat is it? and what vegetables?) The vegetables, well, those my mom puts in the tajine, sweet potatoes, and... I don't remember too well, but they like all kinds of vegetables. And the meat is mostly lamb or chicken."

For disadvantaged parents not from immigration backgrounds, more industrial foods and dishes found in fast-food restaurants appeared in the children's responses, as seen in Antoine's example:

"My dad mostly eats pizzas and hamburgers, four-cheese pizzas. Sometimes soup... Then he likes Whaou pancakes. What else does my dad eat... Well, ham sandwiches with butter, or ham pasta. I think that's all. And my mom eats exactly like my dad."

Several other disadvantaged children stated that they do not know their parents' food preferences well and do not know what their favorite dishes or foods are. The tastes of parents from intermediate and affluent social backgrounds closely resemble those of their children, with the same types of dishes and foods mentioned. **The responses of affluent children were almost always more eclectic, including examples outside the ordinary, such as foreign dishes, rare meats, or uncommonly eaten animals, as well as more variety.** Benjamin recounted:

"My dad likes strange things (he laughs). For example, last Sunday, we had sticky rice, and it's steamed, and it's a kind of Japanese rice. [...] It's very good, but it's a bit strange. Sometimes, he makes sauce with it, and the sauce sticks to the rice, and he makes his sauce with spices; I know he puts curry in it. He likes a lot of weird things like that, Japanese or Chinese things, or Indian things. [...] Yesterday he wasn't working, and he made chicken with bamboo shoots, coconut milk, and yellow spices; it makes a kind of yellow sauce."

Reflections on different consumption practices and habits

According to the children's narratives, it is clear that their overall dietary practices vary greatly depending on their social origins. Thus, **throughout the day and during the four meals, the wealthier the**

children are, the more they eat real whole[179] and varied[180] foods, as well as the less they ingest pathogenic chemical products.

This trend seems just as crucial in social and health issues as it is fraught with consequences! Children of poor parents indeed have daily dietary practices that, in the long run, are likely to promote the development of several chronic diseases, while wealthy children have, on the contrary, a diet that have chances to contribute to their prevention.

These results observed from a sample of forty children do not seem to contrast with those of other research. According to Chantal Julia et al.[181], data from the Nutrinet-Santé study conducted in 2009 with 75,000 French people show that low-income households are overrepresented among consumers of ultra-processed foods, and these foods are also more frequently eaten at a younger age. According to these researchers, the fact that ultra-processed products are more consumed by the poor can be explained because

---

[179] However, this is more of a general trend than a truth that would apply to all foods consumed by children. For example, the fact that children from intermediate social backgrounds consume more "cereals" (for breakfast and ultra-processed) than those who are disadvantaged does not align with the trend we are describing (if positive effects on health are sought, it is clearly better not to consume such products at all, or even skip breakfast altogether, rather than consuming this type of product, especially on a daily basis).

[180] About balance, it is difficult and does not seem relevant to arrive at comparative analyses of children's diets, both according to their social backgrounds and in general. Table No. 9, however, still allows us to observe that disadvantaged children consume significantly fewer fruits and vegetables than other children. The animal products eaten by underprivileged children also appear to mostly come from fast-food restaurants or pre-prepared meals, unlike affluent children who mention various raw meats (sometimes organic) as well as eggs. This helps to understand how a "nutri-centered" conception of the health effects of diet is limited. If, for example, one only focused on the balance between carbohydrates, fats, and proteins when comparing children's diets, one could quickly conclude that they all eat more or less balanced, and therefore, there cannot be any links between dietary habits, social health inequalities, and chronic diseases.

[181] Julia C., Martinez L., Allès B., Touvier M., Hercberg S., Méjean C., Kesse-Guyot E. (2018). Contribution of ultra-processed foods in the diet of adults from the French NutriNet-Santé study. *op.cit.*

they are generally quite inexpensive and already prepared. Similarly, **they attract mainly those with *"low nutritional knowledge."*** According to Laure Schnabel et al.[182], increased consumption of ultra-processed foods is also associated with "low education" (assessed based on the highest diploma obtained).

Table No. 9 presents a summary of typical foods (or the most frequently mentioned foods) that make up the four meals for children: an overall view makes it even more apparent how marked the differences are.

---

182 Schnabel L., Kesse-Guyot E., Allès B., Touvier M., Srour B., Hercberg S., Buscail C., Julia C. (2019). Association Between Ultraprocessed Food Consumption and Risk of Mortality Among Middle-aged Adults in France. *JAMA internal medicine*, 179(4), 490–498. https://doi.org/10.1001/jamainternmed.2018.7289

Table No. 9: Typical foods comprising the four meals of children's day

	Disadvantaged social origins	Intermediate social origins	Affluent social origins
Breakfast	Glass of milk, *Nutella* spread, ultra-processed biscuits, a piece of bread	Glass of milk, *Nutella* spread, a fruit, (ultra-processed) cereals	Bread and jam (organic or homemade), one or two fruits, a yogurt, oat flakes
Lunch (at home)	*Kebabs*, pasta, ham, sausages, pizzas, mashed potatoes, hamburgers	Various dishes and foods, mentions of various vegetables, starches, meats, fish, and legumes	Similar to children of intermediate origins, with the additional mention of organic and homemade
Afternoon snack	Ultra-processed biscuits, soda, *Nutella* spread, bread, candies	Pastries, fruit juice, a fruit	Pastries, fruit juice, a fruit, jam, bread
Dinner	Dishes from the parents' country of origin, pizzas, kebabs, pasta, ham, hamburgers, meals bought at fast-food restaurants	Varied dishes, often homemade soups and broths, different types of vegetables and meats	Similar to children of intermediate origins but with more variety, with the additional mentions of organic and homemade

Some nuances need to be considered in relation to this table. Firstly, I would like to remind that it represents a synthesis of the responses from forty children (as a sample): **it allows us to highlight certain trends, but not to depict the entirety of the social reality regarding the food habits of French children. One might first argue that it is not true that children of workers do not eat fruits, vegetables, and**

quality animal products. Fortunately, reality is more nuanced and complex than what this table summarizes[183].

However, it is true that, out of more than twenty children from disadvantaged social backgrounds who were interviewed, examples of fruits consumed throughout the four meals of the day were mentioned only exceptionally. Similarly, examples of vegetables and meats not from meals purchased at fast-food restaurants were mentioned very little, mostly described as eaten rarely, and mainly in dishes of foreign origin (corresponding to children from immigrant families).

In other words, **my analysis does not claim that disadvantaged children never eat fruits, vegetables, and quality meats, but it does report that, on average, they seem to eat much less of these than children of less poor parents.**

Another nuance, generally applicable to my entire presentation, concerns some limitations regarding the sample that allowed me to arrive at these results. As I have already mentioned in a footnote, all the affluent children I interviewed are also rural children, mostly living in the countryside and attending a school located in the countryside. **It is thus not necessarily evident to assert to what extent certain characteristics of their diet, such as the importance attached to homemade**[184] **food, are related to the relatively affluent situation of their parents or, conversely, to their rurality.** Nevertheless, they are still generally socially affluent (although this is probably not a unidimensional cause-and-effect relationship).

However, there are still some exceptions, including a minority of children from school D whose representations are very similar to those of other affluent children in economic terms but who have

---

[183] I can already anticipate potential remarks like, "I'm a laborer, and my child eats fruits everyday," followed by complete questioning of my entire work.

[184] More precisely, my intuition would associate homemade bread (or for example, *"the bread that dad made,"* as a child mentioned) with a certain rural quality.

parents of middle (or sometimes upper-middle) class and rural background, with a particularly high cultural capital. These exceptions do not invalidate the existence of general trends, although they involve interesting nuances.

This suggests that while food representations seem to correlate with the social positions of parents, they are not strictly "determined" by them, as cultural capital and parental education also play a significant role.

Some ideas mentioned previously through references to other sociological research, particularly about different styles of parental food education, still encourage us to suppose that these traits are at least partially related to social status. This digression may seem anecdotal, but I consider it essential, also to avoid interpreting Table No. 9 or the entirety of my work as devoid of all nuances. With that reflection, let's now return to the issues raised by these results.

These results give me the opportunity to revisit and reaffirm some ideas I had previously developed regarding the budgetary and time constraints related to eating healthily when resources are limited. I had already referred to some researchers who have delved into this subject, some of whom concluded that budgetary constraints condition all modes of food consumption[185].

Such constraints seem to be identified through various aspects in the narratives told by the children. For example, it is the case in the expression by disadvantaged children of often eating "easy" and "quick" meals at home. The act of regularly eating out (kebabs, pizzerias) or buying meals at fast-food restaurants and consuming them at home can also be associated with time constraints (no need to cook) and budget constraints (especially for kebabs which, for less than seven euros, offer a significant quantity of calories at a "lower cost"). This is also the case for what might appear as spatial

---

[185] Ditlevsen K., Halkier B., Holm L. (2022). Pathways of less healthy diets. An investigation of the everyday food practices of men and women in low income households. *op.cit.*

constraints, for example, in the fact that poor parents mostly do their grocery shopping in spaces close to their home compared to affluent parents, or that poor children living in areas where precarity is concentrated frequent fast-food restaurants located near their homes.

However, it is necessary to bring some nuance to deterministic considerations that these constraints would "condition all" food practices.

Firstly, **because a good number of children from the working class have one or both parents who are unemployed and yet eat the same types of easy and quick meals as those whose both parents work** (and are thus even more subject to time constraints, in theory). Secondly, **because not all the foods consumed by disadvantaged children are systematically less expensive than those that other children are accustomed to eating** (although they require more time to prepare). Frequent meals in certain fast-food restaurants can indeed quickly become more expensive than buying and cooking one's own food, without necessarily being less real and varied, by composing balanced meals. These nuances do not mean, however, that budgetary and time constraints do not play a role in these consumption differences, but in my opinion, they should not be the only reasons.

I will propose here the idea that these differences in eating behaviors are also very probably due to different levels of knowledge about the links between food and health, between parents and at least partly according to their social positions. The fact that the stories of some middle-class children whose parents have a high cultural capital are similar to those of affluent children, although they are rather exceptions, shows in a certain way that **income and wealth (or social position) do not entirely determine dietary practices, but that education is also a very important point regarding these practices.**

It has become conventional to associate social inequalities in health correlated with chronic diseases with inequalities in access to healthcare. There are numerous sociological studies highlighting how access to healthcare differs depending on one's professional, geographical, or ethnic situation. I wish, based on the results presented here, to draw attention to **the absolute need to focus more on the relationships between social inequalities in health and disparities in knowledge about the links between nutrition and health, or more generally about what chronic diseases are and how to prevent them**.

This is more of a theory and hypothesis formulated from my work and reasoning than an established and demonstrable fact by other studies. However, the idea of linking social health inequalities related to chronic diseases and disparities in knowledge about chronic diseases and their prevention seems obvious to me, as long as one takes into account the following logic:

1) **Most mentalities are still anchored in the old health paradigm where the fear of infectious diseases dominates that of non-communicable diseases, which are not well understood compared to what they really are and the dangers they represent.**

2) **Knowledge about what chronic diseases are and how to prevent them is not or very little taught in school curricula** (including in French medical faculties, where the specialized branch still called "environmental health" is often sidelined, and where conventional care remains much more studied than prevention[186]). **It is thus acquired more individually and independently.**

3) **As a poorly known and poorly taught subject, it seems logical that the most precarious do not necessarily worry about it, having plenty to do to make ends meet, and that it is the more affluent who have more resources and time to be interested in these issues and challenges.** It is certainly not for nothing that there is a popular

---

[186] Spiroux J. (2007). *Pathologies environnementales*. Paris, Éditions J.Lyon.

idea that "eating organic is a bourgeois thing," and that only in the discourse of socially affluent children do we find the association of "chemical products" with "cancer" or poor health. **The problem is that chronic diseases are not bourgeois problems!**

And this is not a direct criticism addressed to the proletarians and their types of food consumption (because after all, everyone does what they want), but rather a return to the idea that **it is surely high time to do something about education and prevention so that everyone truly knows what they are doing!**[187]

Subsequently, I also asked the children questions about their representations of health, and implicitly about their representations of links between food and health: this should allow us to learn a little more about these disparities in terms of knowledge.

---

[187] Attempting to remain neutral while studying and describing reality as it appears does not necessarily mean wanting things to remain as they are; the distinction between the two is important.

Chapter 6: How children perceive the links between food and health

Representations of health

Children, regardless of their parents' professions, seem to principally associate health with not having an infectious disease and with medical care prescribed by a doctor when they have one. An idea found in almost all children is also that any illness is directly curable by taking medication, after which "*it gets better [...] and it's over.*"

Diabetes, a chronic disease for which insulin injections regulate blood glucose levels, has been equated with an infectious disease, and insulin is seen as the treatment to eradicate the virus, like antibiotics for a throat infection. Similarly, a disadvantaged child whose grandmother had cancer explained, "*It might be because of families, like we can transmit it among ourselves.*" Others also hinted at the idea that cancer, known to them because a family member or acquaintance is affected, can be transmitted like a communicable disease, among other ways, "*through spitting.*"

The only social difference found lies in the fact that several affluent (and rural) children mentioned being accustomed to alternative treatments to medication, such as essential oils, "*plants,*" honey, or herbal teas. Some of them also associated poor health with obesity, stating that obese or overweight people they see on the street "*don't feel good about themselve,*" without being able to explain why they are in poor health.

Without leading to detailed categorizations, the responses nonetheless allowed understanding that **children know very little and poorly understand what chronic diseases are**. This is not surprising, especially because it is relatively rare for them to be affected by such pathologies themselves. It is also entirely possible that parents try to protect their children by not explaining or explaining very little about what their chronically ill relatives actually have. This almost systematic association between health and communicable diseases[188], however, is somewhat worrisome, considering that **these same children will likely face a much higher probability, as adults, of having their living conditions significantly degraded by a chronic disease than by a communicable one...**

I also asked the children to express what, in their opinion, contributes to good health. **Most of them, across the four schools, mentioned the importance of regularly engaging in physical or sports activities or "*often getting fresh air*" to "*move*" and not stay seated in front of screens all the time.** The recurrence of this type of discourse among all children suggests that there is a common awareness, at the elementary school level, of the positive effects of physical activity on health, as well as the detrimental effects of sedentary behavior. **Not smoking and not drinking too much alcohol were also widely mentioned.** In the CM1 classes of schools A and C, teachers dedicate a few hours each year to raise awareness among children about the dangers of tobacco and alcohol.

The association of health with communicable diseases and medications, as well as the importance of physical activity and the harmful effects of tobacco and alcohol, did not appear differently in the children's narratives based on their social backgrounds (although there were still some nuances, such as boys from working-class emphasizing the need to be "muscular" to "be healthy," or that some children from Muslim families explained that alcohol "is bad for health" because it is prohibited in their religion). However, this was not the case when children talked about what concerns food and contributes to good health. And here again, we find discourses that differ significantly based on their social backgrounds.

---

[188] The survey was furthermore conducted in its entirety shortly before the onset of Covid-19. It is likely that the trend I describe here has intensified even more since then.

The first major difference I observed lies in the expression that *"eating five fruits and vegetables"*[189] is *"good for health."* Children often referred to this slogan that they explained seeing on television or in advertisements, but not in the same way. **Disadvantaged children mentioned the five fruits and vegetables a day** (often promoted on French TV) **with mockery and irony, usually laughing. When I asked them why they were laughing and why eating five fruits and vegetables can help maintain good health, some would respond that** *"it's a publicity thing"* **or** *"it's what they say in the fruit and vegetable ads,"* **without being able to explain why this could be good for health.** It seems that, for them, it was about creating an amusing interaction with me by referring to a well-known advertisement, but that **this slogan had no meaning for them.**

And this is also a general conclusion that can be drawn from this research as a whole: **slogans do not seem to work with children regarding diet awareness if they are not accompanied by detailed explanations.** In contrast, when they spoke about the five fruits and vegetables a day, children from intermediate and affluent social backgrounds were not joking, were not ironic, and developed explanations about the benefits of this behavior. Here is, for example, part of the response from Matteo, ten years old, whose father is a site manager, and mother is a teacher, director, and founder[190] of school D, when I asked him how to maintain good health:

"Well, we have to eat about five fruits and vegetables... Per day! Otherwise, if it's per week, well, it's not enough. For our parents, it's not at all enough, so it's better per day. And don't eat too many candies... Everything that is cakes, ice creams... And also avoid hamburgers because they are bad... Everything that is too fatty and

---

[189] This is a slogan that has been promoted for years in France, especially on TV.
[190] Parents with social positions that are somewhat intermediate, with demonstrations of a particularly high cultural capital (I also interviewed them in a semi-structured interview).

chemical, actually. Well, the hamburgers we make ourselves, with pickles from the garden, they're good! When we know what we put in, well, it's for sure better, well, it's not bad... For health. And so, conversely, when we eat something we didn't make ourselves, well, we don't know if there are things that are not good in it. (Prompt: you said we have to eat five fruits and vegetables a day, for what purpose?) *Because it's full of vitamins! Your body needs it!"*

The ironically mentioned five fruits and vegetables a day represent the only association between diet and what contributes to good health for disadvantaged children. Those from intermediate social backgrounds spoke about the importance of "eating balanced" and having enough vegetables, not eating "too sweet" and "too salty," or "not too much fast food." According to Théo:

"You shouldn't eat too much fast food... [...] Fries are super salty, everything we eat in fast food is salty, and not just a little. You can eat it from time to time, but you shouldn't eat it every day. (Follow-up: why?) *So as not to get fat!"*

Affluent children again spoke about the importance of not *"eating chemicals in food,"* *"trying to eat organic,"* and *"not eating things we don't know what's in them."*

The differences between the narratives of children from intermediate and affluent backgrounds refer to what I presented earlier as the different fears of parents about the effects of diet on their children's health (see Table No. 4): **in the sense that the former seem to be more concerned about quantitative limitations, while the latter are more concerned about the quality of food.**

Table No. 10: Different representations of what contributes to good health related to diet, according to the interviewed children

	Disadvantaged social origins	Intermediate social origins	Affluent social origins
Representations of what enables good health in connection with food	"Eat five fruits and vegetables a day" was the only example going in that direction, expressed ironically and with laughter, without being able to explain it.	Not eating too much sugar, too much salt, or too much fat to avoid gaining weight; Limiting fast food; Eating five fruits and vegetables a day	Not ingesting "chemicals" or products with unknown composition, eating organic and homemade, consuming fruits and vegetables

Health education

Regarding the question "what have they told you at school about health?" the responses echoed some characteristics already mentioned, such as the fact that children from school A and school B have already been sensitized to tobacco and alcohol consumption, and to a lesser extent, it seems, to the importance of physical activity. A child from school B explained that in her CM1 class, the teacher preferred not to address health at all to avoid "hurting" certain students whose family members suffer from cancer or other serious illnesses.

In school D, children told me that the director had already invited a naturopath to talk about health: "He talked about what to eat and what is good for health, and also about our bodies, how they work."

However, it was only a single intervention for a few hours, and it is clear that the children remembered more the man's friendliness than the knowledge he presented. It is highly likely that such a single, non-recurring intervention is not enough to anchor real knowledge in their minds.

The responses to the question "what have your parents told you about health?" seem more eloquent to fuel the analysis. It is interesting, for example, to note that out of twenty children interviewed in schools A and B, Nelson was the only one to talk about food. He, also the only child from these schools whose parents hold affluent positions, recounted that his parents regularly ask him and his siblings, among other things, to: "*Eat well-balanced and pay attention to what we eat and drink.*" The responses of disadvantaged children consisted more of examples of good behavior, such as "*dressing warmly when it's cold,*" "*eating with the right hand*" (for some Muslim children), or "*wearing glasses properly and taking care of them.*"

Children from intermediate social backgrounds often referred to the fact that their parents ask them to eat balanced and "*not always eat the same thing,*" while affluent children, not surprisingly, again mentioned chemicals, organic, and the idea that it is necessary to "*be very careful about what we eat.*"

In general, **it emerges that the more socially affluent children are, not only do their parents talk to them more about food, but they explicitly do so more in connection with health**. Julie explained, "*Every night, they tell me you have to eat this, you haven't eaten enough of that. What did you eat? They want to know everything all the time* (laughs). *But well... I know it's for my good, so I listen to them.*"

We can also conclude that poor parents do not integrate, or very little, food dimension into the health education they transmit to their children. This is also evident when considering their representations of the meaning of the expression "eating well."

What does eating well mean

I will present here, as the final results of the interviews with children, the responses to the questions: "in your opinion, what does eating well mean?" and "what is eating poorly?". Again, their answers differ significantly depending on the positions occupied by their parents.

There are mainly two types of content in the responses of children of poor parents: the association of eating well with respect for the Muslim religion, as well as not wasting food.

According to Kasim, nine years old, who identified as "Turkish," whose both parents are from Turkey and unemployed, eating well is not:

"Leaving the plate with half of it, or not respecting your food. Dirtying the food, for example, if I put alcohol in the plate pretending it's olive oil, it's dirty! And it's haram. And leaving half on the plate is not good, we pay with money. Also, it's about respect, not dirtying, eating with the right hand, eating everything properly."

Similar associations between "dirty" and consumption of foods prohibited by the Muslim religion were made by several children, including Samba, who explained that eating well is eating "good" and "clean" things, meaning not eating dirty things prohibited by Islam (*"pork is dirty, it rolls in the mud and eats anything"*). **But eating well was mainly linked by disadvantaged children to not wasting and *"finishing your plate properly."* It is, in fact, about respecting the expense that parents have made to feed their children.** According to Mélanie, whose dad is a mover, and mom is unemployed, eating well is:

"For example, pizza, spaghetti, that for example is eating well, especially with a good appetite. Eating well is when you finish everything on your plate, you don't leave a crumb. Otherwise at home, well sometimes you can't leave the table if you don't finish

everything. (Prompt: why?) Well, there are some who have nothing to eat at all... And then dad works hard to buy what we eat."

The expression of the importance of not wasting food was also often followed by table manners, such as *"eating properly and not getting it everywhere," "not making a mess," "sitting up straight,"* or *"not eating the whole dish alone and sharing with others."* **The narratives of what eating well means for disadvantaged children seem to mainly reflect the fear of scarcity, as well as the economic constraints that make waste unthinkable**[191]. For Paola, *"eating well is necessarily eating a lot, to make sure you're not too hungry afterward"*.

Eating well was never associated even once with the question of waste by children from intermediate social backgrounds. Their responses were very similar to each other; they generally consisted of the assertion that eating well is above all "*eating balanced*" and "*not eating too much*." Cassandra's statements illustrate this trend quite well:

"Eating well is having enough vegetables to make it balanced, starches, meat, fruits, cheese. If we don't take an appetizer, well, we can have salad before the cheese. (I follow up: so what is eating balanced then?) *It's eating everything, varying what you eat, not always the same thing.* (Prompt: why is it important to eat balanced?) *Well, not to get fat, it's important not to get fat* (Follow-up: why?) *To stay well, not be fat* (she laughs). (Prompt: so being fat means not being well?) *It can cause problems for people...* (Follow-up: why?) *Well... I don't know."*

It was also sometimes about not eating *"too sweet or too salty,"* or *"not eating too much at McDonald's, otherwise... you'll get fat and end up too big!"*

---

[191] However, it is interesting to note that during observations of school canteen meals, it was these same children who tended to generate the most food waste (especially avoiding the served vegetables).

Among affluent children (and incidentally, from parents with intermediate social positions but benefiting from significant cultural capital), the need to vary one's diet was still present, but the reference to eating balanced was less frequently used. **The purpose of varying one's diet was no longer to avoid getting fat but "*to be healthy.*"** For exemple, according to Samantha:

"*Eating well is not eating only what you really like but what is good for your body. For example, for starters, you can have tomatoes with sauce, for the main course, steak with spinach, then for dessert, you can have a fruit and yogurt. Only occasionally an ice cream.* (Prompt: you said 'what is good for your body,' can you explain what you mean?) *If we eat, for example, chips and candies and more chips and candies, well, that's not good, not good for the body. To eat well, it's not just about vegetables, but a little bit of everything, vegetables then meat then ice cream, um... you still have to eat vegetables every day! For mom, if we haven't eaten any vegetables today, it's horrible, horrible, really horrible! So we have to eat vegetables every day, and for her, eating well is organic vegetables and more vegetables*".

The responses of affluent children again differed by incorporating organic and homemade aspects into their discourse, as well as "chemicals." Apolline asserted that eating well is "*eating good things.*" When asked what these good things correspond to, she explained:

"*When we take a fruit, well, it's better to take a fruit that is organic. Otherwise, when we take fruits or vegetables from the garden, they are bigger and better. Also, my mom often prefers to make dishes because when we buy ready-made dishes, we don't know what's really in them... so there can be bad things.* (Prompt: bad things? What is that?) *Bad things, for example, chemicals, well, chemical things. That's bad* (Follow-up: why?) *Well, over time, it can cause problems, or even diseases*".

The responses of affluent children were always longer and more detailed than those of others, and once again accompanied by explanations and justifications. They systematically associated the expression "eating well" with health, with sentences emphasizing the need to pay attention to the quality of their food.

Distrust of what is not homemade or what is industrial was here a bit more developed by Benjamin, testifying to some rather advanced knowledge of what food additives are and their harmful effects. According to Benjamin (aged nine), eating poorly corresponds to:

"Eating only junk... things that are not good for health (Follow-up: and what is not good for health, the junk? *Those things from supermarkets, things like that. Most of the things from the supermarket, actually.* (Follow-up: why?) *They put a lot of products to make it last longer, well, longer, and it's not good for health and not good for nature. And it even tastes better... They put products in it that make you think it tastes better, but no, not at all, it puts an effect in your head, when you realize that it's not normal. They also do it so that you eat a lot and you have the impression that it's good, but when afterward you taste a normal vegetable, you realize that it's not the same and that it's done on purpose to take a lot. And you think it tastes better when it doesn't already, it doesn't taste better and besides, it's not good for health"*.

Table No. 11 allows summarizing again the categories established from these results.

Table No. 11: Different representations and discourses about what eating well means

	Disadvantaged social origins	Intermediate social origins	Affluent social origins
Means	Not wasting, "respecting" food, good table manners, sharing what we eat	Eating balanced and varied, not 'too sweet or salty,' limiting the visits to and consumption of fast food	Eat organic and homemade, have a varied diet, avoid processed foods and additives
Quantity and quality	Eati enough	Not overeat	Eat foods considered "good for health"
Fears	Lack of food or having it go to waste	Becoming "too big" (which leads to poor health)	"Chemicals" or unidentified products, additives, lack of quality
Types of narratives	Short and descriptive	Intermediate, sometimes and partially explanatory	Long and explanatory

The stakes of different representations of health and about the links between food and health

Associating eating well with accessing a sufficient quantity of food, as observed in children from poor families, reflects a certain valuation and concern for abundance, most likely marked by experiences of deprivation within families. **Subsistence seems to be the absolute priority**, while most values mentioned, such as the importance of "respecting" food, can be linked to an economic and material necessity for parents to teach their children not to waste.

It has long been known that representations of health and the body vary according to social classes, so people from the working class tend to attach less importance to health as a value, as well as to related consumption[192]. **Eating well appears here as linked to the need to stay alive immediately, either through access to quantity, rather than maintaining good health in the long term**. As specified by Scrinis[193], the poorest are mainly concerned with accessing a sufficient quantity of calories, regardless of their quality.

However, according to all the interviews I conducted with disadvantaged children, **it seems unlikely that they themselves have experienced real episodes of deprivation or have actually lacked food in quantity[194]. It is, however, very likely, although it is only a theory, that this fear of shortage has been transmitted to them by their families, similarly to what is called habitus.**

The desire to "not eat too much," to limit sugar and salt consumption (as well as meals purchased in fast-food restaurants) among children from intermediate social backgrounds can be identified as a set of representations of eating well related to the effects of food on health. However, **the health dimension of eating well seems to be more or less reduced to a quantitative limitation of food and the fear of overweight and obesity, which has probably also been transmitted to children by their parents.**

In more affluent children, concerns about the effects of food on health are more related to quality than quantity. The fear of "eating too much" is not so much mentioned, replaced by the fear of ingesting foods that would contain additives or ingredients whose composition cannot be clearly identified. The claim for

---

[192] Boltanski L. (1971), Les usages sociaux du corps. *Annales*, 26-1, 205-233.

[193] Scrinis G. (2013). *Nutrisionism - The Science and Politics of Dietary Advice. op.cit.*

[194] Except for Yaprak, a Turkish child who arrived in France with her family a few months before the interview, whose parents seemed extremely poor, and she evidently did not eat much. (She explained having her first meal of the day after 4:30 PM, just a piece of bread with tea).

organic and homemade seems, in fact, to stem from a significant desire to control one's diet, especially regarding its potential effects on health.

It is thus possible to assert that **the more affluent the social origins of children, but also the more parents seem to benefit from a high cultural capital, the more they conceptualize the notion of eating well with concerns related to health**.

These three types of conceptions correspond to increasing orders of importance for healthy eating: as presented in the section dedicated to what constitutes healthy eating, the quality of one's food consumption is more important than controlling its quantity, just as varying one's diet and eating balanced do not provide real added value if one does not consume real and whole foods. Also, to a lesser extent, controlling the quantity of one's nutrition is still preferable to associating abundance with good health[195]. Especially if our consumption includes a majority of ultra-processed foods, as is the case with the disadvantaged children interviewed.

---

[195] Quantitative caloric abundance is undoubtedly essential in a context where obtaining food is difficult, but it rather poses a danger in the era of food industrialization (especially when coupled with poor food quality).

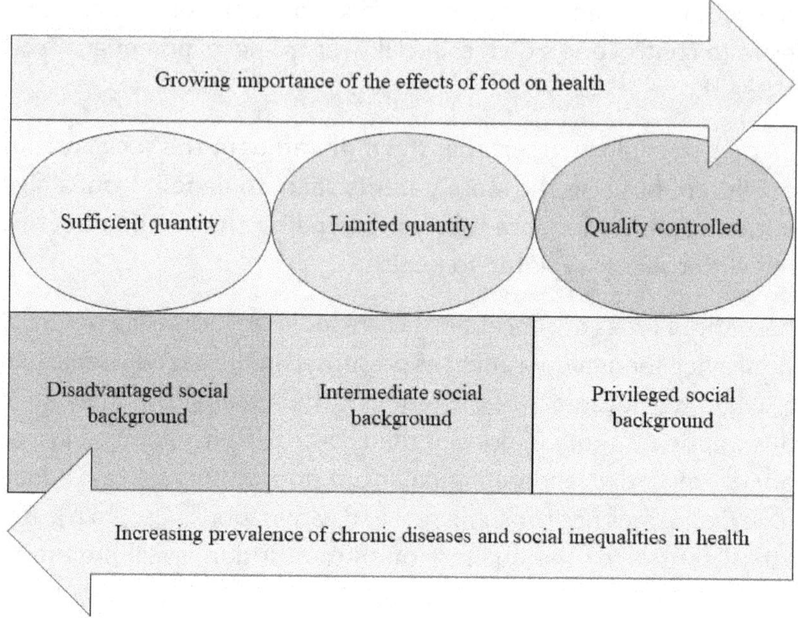

Figure No. 2: Health and social stakes of different representations of the effects of food on health

This is, of course, the presentation of a general trend, not a systematic reality (applying to all individuals or children based on their parents' professions). It is undoubtedly good to reiterate; there is no intention to hierarchize dietary practices or to denounce "poor" populations that eat "poorly" and applaud "rich" ones that eat "well." Instead, the aim is to consider avenues highlighting potential reasons for the simultaneous increase in the prevalence of chronic diseases and social inequalities in health.

Chapter 7: Survey implications and theories

The results presented in this section have allowed an understanding of trends regarding the food representations and practices of children, and indirectly, their parents as educators and eaters. Although the interviews that facilitated these observations also covered other topics, it seems unnecessary to continue the exposition, as the children's narratives are becoming repetitive, leading to information saturation.

This redundancy reinforces the reliability of the proposed categorizations.

A global look at these categories leads me to assert that children's relationships with food are highly likely, in the long term[196], to be vectors of important social inequalities in health. In other words, and as I have previously stated, the poorer the children's backgrounds, the more likely their relationships with food are to make them ill.

I think this is not only true for children but for the entire population. Children, based on the connections between their tastes, representations, practices, and the food education they receive, seem to be mirrors of different food habitus relative to social classes or positions within society.

The concept of habitus, often used in sociology, makes sense as a theoretical path to explain variations in these relationships with food[197], as **children have demonstrated the internalization of sets**

---

[196] Chronic diseases rarely occur in childhood but rather develop over time through a gradual decline in health.

[197] See also our article in Health Sociology Review: Lebredonchel L. Fardet A. (2022). How French children food representations and tastes vary according to their social backgrounds: a study of disparities in food habitus. *Health Sociology Review*, online publication https://doi.org/10.1080/14461242.2022.2148832

of representations and norms that contribute to shaping their tastes, likely persisting over time.

According to Pierre Bourdieu, *"Habitus generates distinct and distinctive practices...; but they are also classificatory schemes, principles of classification, principles of vision and division of different tastes. They make differences between what is good and what is bad, between what is right and what is wrong, between what is distinguished and what is vulgar, etc"*. [198] They are also *"powerful factors of social reproduction"* and class differences (*"each, by obeying his 'personal taste,' by realizing his individual project, agrees spontaneously and unknowingly with thousands of others who think, feel, and choose like him[199]."*)

Bourdieu already proposed the idea that it is possible to distinguish several types of habitus in contemporary French society, resulting in the existence of three main "lifestyles." These are defined by a *"set of tastes, beliefs, and systematic practices characteristic of a class or fraction of a given class. It includes, for example, political opinions, moral convictions, aesthetic preferences, but also sexual and dietary practices"*.[200] **Bourdieu's theory of a French society with three distinct lifestyles, according to habitus related to social position, seems to particularly coincide with the three categories of children based on their tastes and representations.**

According to this, **the habitus of individuals from the working class is mainly based on adaptation to necessity, which involves a taste for what is perceived as favorable to survival, within a context of constraints.** Some food sociologists refer to the tastes of the poorest

---

[198] Bourdieu P. (1994). *Raisons pratiques. Sur la théorie de l'action*. Paris, Éditions du Seuil.

[199] *Ibid.*

[200] *Ibid.*

as a *"taste of necessity."*[201] Similarly, the working class values strength because physical labor generally represents a condition for its survival.

Necessity can thus be associated with a need for foods that provide a significant quantity of calories at a lower cost. In his research, Bourdieu also observed that the working class favors foods that give them strength in the short term, while the "dominant classes" are more concerned about their health in the long term[202]. The problem remains that these calorie-rich foods that "give strength" in the short term are often ultra-processed and industrial products, which weaken and make people sick over time.

As for the "dominant classes" (according to Bourdieu), their habitus is based on strategies and logics of "distinction": that is, distinguishing themselves from other classes by having exclusive practices that mark differences, contributing to establishing their lifestyle. Those Bourdieu called "the petite bourgeoisie," or the middle class, are somewhat caught between the "dominant" and the "working" classes, trying to both rise socially and distinguish themselves from the latter while also facing certain constraints. It is also interesting to note that, similar to the fact that children from intermediate social backgrounds often speak of the importance of not "eating too much," Bourdieu had noticed that the habitus of *"the petite bourgeoisie"*[203] was partly based on restriction.

The numerous similarities between the results of my survey and the concept of habitus in Bourdieu's sociology lead to the idea that the

---

[201] Oncini F. (2019). Feeding distinction: Economic and cultural capital in the making of food boundaries. *Poetics,* 73, 17-31. https://doi.org/10.1016/j.poetic.2019.02.002

[202] Bourdieu P. (1979). *La Distinction : critique sociale du jugement. op.cit.*

[203] I place this expression in quotation marks and use it to refer to Bourdieu, although I prefer to talk about the middle or intermediate class, as the term "petite bourgeoisie" seems somewhat tinged with a pejorative connotation and does not always correspond to the reality on the ground.

fundamental differences I observed regarding children's nutrition correspond to food habitus.

This is not without consequence, implying that **the representations and practices I have described are probably not unique to children, but are ingrained as habitus, enduring and likely to remain similar once they become adults.**

In a way, **the trends I have described are most probably not only true for children but for the entire society.** This would imply that, following this reasoning, **the more socially disadvantaged individuals are, the more likely all their relationships with food are to make them ill.**

This proposition is somewhat contradictory, given that it seems evident that **food consumption, although highly influenced by cultural factors, is an activity originally oriented toward survival and the life of the species. This holds true for every people or social group, as the cultural factors of food consumption actually correspond to practices designed to optimize life and survival based on the edible resources available in a given territory, compatible with its environment, climate, biodiversity, and the demographics of the humans inhabiting it.** How can these practices become more destructive[204] than favorable to life?

It is evident that the "taste for necessity," or for inexpensive foods that contain the greatest possible quantities of calories, must have originated in a context of repeated experiences of deprivation and limited access to nutrition. The industrialization of nutrition, followed by the arrival of supermarkets and hypermarkets since the 1950s in France, tended to limit, if not eradicate, for the majority of the French population, the scarcity of access to nutrition in quantity.

Despite the end of this scarcity and quantitative deprivation, the food habitus of the working classes has persisted and continued to

---

[204] This term may indeed seem a bit strong, but the word seems justified to describe a daily diet that is likely to undermine health.

be transmitted from parents to children, retaining the characteristics for which it appeared (although the context has changed).

Understanding this phenomenon has allowed me to conceive a more general theory concerning culture, norms, and group identity. **I will first revisit and develop the idea that each set of food habits, which we can also call "food cultures," is based on what was originally available within a given territory, depending on its living conditions.** This includes soil fertility, exposure to sunlight, climate, temperature, water, weather, as well as demographics.

These food habits also rely on what promotes the survival of the group inhabiting this territory. Precisely because they are favorable to the survival of the group, they form its food culture and are so ingrained that they become part of its identity, even evolving into habitus. This partly explains why most communities of foreign origins or minorities living in a country that is not where their ancestors lived tend to retain a set of d food habits specific to their country of origin, as these are important to their identity, even though the foods defining these habits are sometimes not available in the new occupied territory (originally, without importation).

According to this logic, **culture is based on practices that were favorable to the survival of a group in a given environment, sufficiently long for these practices to integrate the identity of this group, being transmitted by parents and education.**

I will propose the theory that **culture, as a major participant in shaping the identity of a group because it is based on practices favorable to its survival, persists over time well beyond the material conditions in which it took shape, even becoming a threat to the survival of the same group.**

In other words, the "socially constructed" is based on what is available in a given environment and promotes the survival of a group or society long enough (to root itself as the foundation of its identity) and endures far beyond the context in which it was "constructed."

This also leads to the assertion that **identity is formed primarily based on what is favorable to the survival of a group, to the point where it can then prevail over that survival**. These are complex and speculative[205] theories that somewhat extend the scope of my work on nutrition.

To return to the main topic, these ideas assimilate to the notion that **the food habitus of disadvantaged individuals is based on the culture of practices that were once beneficial, if not essential, to their survival and persist, even though these same practices are now deleterious.**

This seems to be explained by the fact that changes related to the industrialization of food, including the degradation of matrices during ultra-processing, are recent and have come very rapidly. Their effects on health are not only poorly known by society at large but especially by the poor.

It is by no means certain that parents would feed their children in the same way if they were more aware of the effects of ultra-processed foods, or the act of ingesting daily degraded or destroyed matrices, nutrient remnants devoid of quality, and pathogenic additives.

One might argue that humans are complex beings who sometimes engage in behaviors that are harmful to themselves while being well aware of their harmfulness, such as daily smoking over several months or years.

However, **a certain anthropological or universal ethics dictates that cigarettes should not be given to children, and they should not be encouraged to smoke. In other words, adults have the right to**

---

[205] They are also unconventional and could even be interpreted as controversial, in part because they do not align with a historical interpretation focused on relations of domination.

deteriorate themselves as individuals[206], but must leave their children the opportunity to be healthy to decide their own fates later.**

This reasoning implies that it is essential to transmit, at least to children, a food education that provides them with all the information they need to make consumption choices that will not make them unhealthy. These will allow them, in turn, as adults, to benefit from knowledge that will help them be more attentive to the diet of their own children.

Forcing parents to provide food education conducive to the health of their children is not conceivable or possible, as parents would need to be educated first, and it is logical that an adult, especially a parent, would not accept rules about how to educate their children. **I see only two remaining types of solutions**.

The first, as I have already presented the idea, would initially be to limit the marketing of ultra-processed foods or even ban them altogether, which, despite sounding a bit radical, seems entirely coherent. Then, secondly, to impose stricter regulation on intensive agriculture and farming (use of chemical fertilizers, pesticides, and other harmful products for both human health and the environment). This kind of solution would have the merit of compelling a true and pathogen-free diet, likely solving the majority of current health problems related to food.

However, all of this would require too significant political, economic, and societal changes to remain realistic and not be considered utopian. It would indeed require moving away from our liberal system (at least for agribusiness), as well as a complete revaluation

---

206 While it's not as simple as that: taking the case of daily smoking, it will not only affect the health of the adult but also that of their future children (if conceived subsequently to their smoking). Sperm and eggs are cells, and thus are not exempt from the cellular degradation caused by smoking (and even if this has not yet been observed empirically or "scientifically proven," it is likely that an increased deleterious diet would have a similar effect, as what is ingested constantly interacts with all cells).

of the professions of farmers and breeders. (This would involve being willing to pay a little more for food and remunerate farmers, agriculturalists, and breeders who contribute to the production of healthful foods, even if it means restricting other usual expenses. And, above all, significantly reducing the margins of intermediaries who buy from producers at very low costs to resell to supermarkets, pocketing a substantial profit without producing any real value.)

Although these proposals seem fair and legitimate to me, they remain utopian. I have not done all this work for it to end with political clichés resembling pub conversations like "they should to this...," or with ideas too unrealistic to have any chance of leading to something concrete.

The second type of solution is this time realistic, concretely and directly applicable (provided it is eventually taken into account by the government): **the implementation of food education in schools, commensurate with all the issues I have presented so far.** The legitimacy of such a measure no longer seems questionable, so the question now is not why but how?

Another alternative solution, more limited, is individual or small-scale awareness that it is time to change our perspective on food and our practices. Unfortunately, its scope is far too small to lead to real societal changes but remains fundamental: it is about small changes from the bottom, from the people. I hope that my contribution, modest as it may be, will have the opportunity to contribute to this approach, even if it only reaches a handful of people.

Part 3: What solutions?

Chapter 8: Food education in schools as a solution for significant top-down changes

You have probably understood that food education in schools appears to be one of the most viable solutions in our current context to combat social health inequalities and the rise of chronic diseases through nutrition. However, this is still a broad field, offering numerous possibilities in both form and content. The fact that food education in schools is not currently mandatory in France, and there is no real program or set of guidelines provided to teachers, leads to a multitude of practices.

In the course of my work, I also explored how to propose a functional and coherent food education in schools that can effectively address the mentioned objectives. I attempted to combine theoretical analyses with the results of my survey, leading to small experiments with CM1 and CM2 classes in schools A, B, C, and D. This chapter will present what I have learned and discovered through this part of the research. While I don't have high expectations regarding actions and resources deployed by officials based on this contribution, I still prefer to share the results of my work (in case it could still be useful, even abroad[207] or in a distant future).

---

[207] During a meeting with members of the regional office for Africa of the World Health Organization, due to their interest in one of my research articles, I noticed that other countries are facing a situation similar to France regarding food education. The context is more or less the same in Congo and several African countries: obesity and diet-related chronic diseases are on the rise, but there is no formal program or institutionalization of food education in schools (despite independent associative initiatives). Members of the WHO African office seemed quite surprised to learn that France is exactly in the same situation.

The proposals and small experiments I implemented for a functional and coherent food education were also designed in opposition to what doesn't work and lacks coherence. I will begin my presentation with this aspect.

I would like to emphasize that my research focused entirely on elementary schools, although some observations I made are likely valid for middle school as well. In my opinion, elementary schools have the advantage of not yet dividing teachings, as is the case in middle school with one teacher per subject. This represents an opportunity to move from the most general (in elementary school) to the more specific (in secondary education). I will revisit this point later.

What doesn't work or lack coherence in food education at school

Slogans and injunctions

As I have already explained through several examples, such as "eat five fruits and vegetables a day," as well as posters against food waste scattered in the cafeteria of school B, **slogans, especially those with an injunctive tone, do not seem to work with children at school to raise awareness or educate them about the links between food and health**[208].

An explanation that can be proposed for this observation is to refer to the idea of "cultural distance,"[209] which, according to sociologists

---

[208] Certainly not at school. As for family or parental food education, it has not been demonstrated that injunctions do not work, especially if they are consistent with the daily practices to which children are exposed. Moreover, the food habits of children from affluent social backgrounds, who have chances of contributing to maintaining good health, seem to be built not only from explanations provided by their parents, which are undoubtedly fundamental, but also from strict control and injunctions.

[209] Dozon J.P., Fassin D. (2001). *Critique de la santé publique*. Paris, Balland.

164

Dozon and Fassin, arises when health-related discourses do not take into account the culture of the populations they address. It is easy to imagine that in practice, these are often precarious populations, the most affected by health problems, and therefore the most likely to be targeted by such messages. And this is not a mere theoretical consideration that I would assert after reading and being influenced by certain ideologies, but a coherent explanation based on what I have observed in the field!

Also noted by Aurélie Maurice[210] with young middle school students: **the resistance generated among students by imperative forms of food education seems to express a certain gap between what they are told to do, what is "good," and their daily eating practices**. In other words, to achieve effectiveness, it appears that educating about food, which involves intimacy and identity, is not done in the same way as teaching mathematics, which pertains more to objective and school-related knowledge, where subjectivities are not involved.

Once again, **the purpose is not to highlight these arguments to advocate for ideologies wishing to abolish everything related to injunctions,** or to promote a conception of children as kings to whom adults should bow. Instead, **it is an attempt to be as pragmatic as possible regarding what I have observed in the field.**

This also presents difficulties, implying that a certain adaptation to children seems necessary to educate about nutrition. The main danger here would be to fall into a kind of relativism, affirming that each child's daily eating practices are very good and perfectly healthy, which is absolutely undesirable.

There is also little interest in educating about nutrition, with the aim of long-term health effects, by teaching children that "there

---

[210] Maurice A. (2014). *Les préadolescents comme ressorts des actions de santé publique : Analyse d'un projet d'éducation alimentaire en collège*. [Thèse de doctorat, Université de Paris]. https://www.theses.fr/2014PA05H008

are no bad foods"[211], **or by disproportionately emphasizing the pleasure of eating at the expense of health**. This is an idea that I have already seen implemented and is also evident in some associative (or commercial) approaches to food education, which I will not mention here, where children quickly end up tasting a bit of everything in class under the pretext of "food education."

Another risk is to encourage separatist practices that, by seeking to valorize specific food cultures of disadvantaged or foreign-origin children, would also deviate from the health dimension and become more of an education in living together through food.

The opposite, not considering certain differences in food cultures and the practices that this implies to have the most universal and general message possible, would also risk losing a portion of the children, most likely the most disadvantaged. This would, of course, limit the interest of the approach by restricting the fight against social inequalities in health through nutrition. As you have understood, the situation is delicate and complex.

Another explanation for the inefficiency of slogans is that they seem to resemble orders given by adults (similarly to "clean your room!"), providing no room for understanding for children. According to this (mis-)understanding of the child receiving the message, applying the injunction of the slogan will correspond to obeying the adults, and not applying it to disobedience. In other words, **children's ability to understand their own interests in responding to slogans or injunctions appears to be very limited, if not nonexistent.**

---

[211] According to Report No. 84 from the French National Council of Food, dedicated to food education at school (see: https://cna-alimentation.fr/download/avis-n84-education-a-lalimentation/). This is not a systematic critique of this report, which includes aspects that are very interesting and relevant in my view, but rather a warning about a certain tendency towards relativism in current developments, which does not seem compatible with the idea of food education for health.

What if we tried to involve the children? For example, by giving them a voice and encouraging them to mobilize their knowledge and talk about their habits **while guiding their speeches to make them think about the links between food and health?** Both without making them feel guilty about detrimental health behaviors they may have, but also by attempting to explain that some practices are preferable to others and why.

In theory, children's participation could, through expression, prevent them from feeling excluded by vertical messages that do not take into account their identity (which is known to be linked to eating habits) and with which they would not feel concerned.

It is partly on this reflection, attempting to integrate the various issues I have presented, that I based some experiments. I will come back to these later after addressing other aspects of what doesn't work and lacks coherence.

Taste classes and other practical initiatives moving away from the health dimension

The taste class is an approach recommended by the French Ministry of National Education and sometimes implemented in certain schools (always based on individual, associative, or community initiatives but not mandatory and not controlled by academic inspectors). According to a joint report from the French Ministry of National Education and the French Ministry of Agriculture:

"The school must enable every student to acquire the knowledge and skills essential to adopt dietary behaviors relevant to their health and the environment, in a process of individual and collective responsibility."[212] According to this report, the "taste class operation" is "*implemented in many primary schools as part of*

---

[212] French Ministry of Education and French Ministry of Agriculture and Food. (2018). Report "Éducation alimentaire de la jeunesse".

partnerships," as well as the "taste week," "*also well-established in practices and implemented in most territories*."

The main problem with these "operations," in my opinion, is that they provide too few guidelines and advice to teachers regarding their objectives and how to achieve them. On paper, one of the central objectives is, of course, health, but **in practice, the lack of provided information, as well as the fact that the recommendations remain very broad, can quickly lead to a considerable distance from the health dimension**.

It is possible that teachers may be sensitive to the issue of nutrition, as well as full of goodwill and good intentions (undoubtedly required to conduct optional "education about" sessions in parallel with already overloaded school programs and often overcrowded classes), but they may not have sufficiently rich knowledge about the links between food and health.

Such initiatives are interesting, especially because being able to taste foods in class or sometimes even participate in the preparation of small dishes helps expand children's food repertoires, exposing them to more variety. However, it remains that not all variety is good for health, and expanding one's food repertoire with unhealthy products is not meaningful in the context of food education. What I write here may seem obvious, but it still deserves to be explicitly formulated, given some situations I have observed in the field, as well as according to certain accounts from interviewed children and teachers.

As a reminder, School A, where I conducted part of the survey, is located in a priority neighborhood of the city. It is mainly attended by children of working-class and unemployed parents, evolving in sometimes very precarious environments. These children are also mostly of immigrant descent, either through their parents or grandparents. The neighborhood is poor and tough. The school is not exempt from this context: violence among children is quite significant, and fights and conflicts among students are frequent.

Every year, a teacher from School A organizes the "taste week"; she says she is particularly concerned about food education, as well as sensitive to this subject. She invests her personal time and a lot of energy into it. The principle is as follows: during one week, children are encouraged to bring, every day, in turn, a food or dish from home (implicitly from their parents' country of origin) or one that is dear to them. It can then be tasted and shared by all the children in the class. The child who brings this dish is also invited to present it to the others. This is also what the children of School A explained to me when they talked about the taste week. According to Anouar:

"Oh yes, the taste week is that each child, well, it's not mandatory, but each child has to bring dishes from home. So I brought gazelle horns, Arabian cakes, star-shaped cakes, what are they called again? I don't remember... Anyway, oh yes, we put Smarties on them and little things of all colors, we put that on the cakes."

In this situation, the taste week seems much more like an education in living together through food than a food education, in the sense that concerns about the effects of food on health seem completely absent (or well hidden).

However, the teacher seemed to think that she was implementing the recommendations for the "taste week" as proposed by the national education system, as well as considering her approach as related to the desire to practice food education at school. It remains to be questioned what knowledge about nutrition that could benefit the health of future adults will be gained from the consumption of *Smarties* and other "colorful things on cakes". And do not be mistaken; it would be too easy to blame the teacher, who is only trying to do what she can with what she has. However, it is indeed a concrete example of what can result from a taste class or week, with the little guidance and advice that educational staff currently have.

This may again be seen as obvious, **but it is essential that these types of practical food education initiatives,** including taste classes and weeks, cooking workshops, etc., **fit into a coherent framework and are based on relevant considerations about what constitutes healthy eating**. It is also fundamental that these considerations regarding what constitutes healthy eating include the understanding that quality is more important than quantity (of nutrients), as well as knowledge of the matrix effect or the consequences of ultra-processing.

Otherwise, not only will they not be relevant, but they will also resemble a relativistic context from which any drift will be possible. This includes, for example, the possibility of allowing representatives of a food company to enter the school to promote its ultra-processed products, with degraded matrices and filled with additives, by teaching children that these are "good for health" because they contain all the "nutrients they need" to "meet their nutritional needs."

There is also a widespread idea that certain foods should not be "demonized," most often referring to products that are bad for health, under the pretext that "pleasure" is something important in nutrition. This kind of communication strategy is probably effective in marketing but certainly has no place in the context of food education! Or it quickly leads to the absurd tasting of deleterious products under the guise of "education," which is absolutely pointless.

Starting with a nutri-centric approach for children

I have already criticized several times the "nutri-centric" approach to the effects of nutrition on health, in other words, the fact of mainly or only considering nutritional balance, excluding or minimizing the importance of the matrix effect and the degree of food processing, or simply put, the quality of food[213]. Again, this does not mean that I question the importance of nutritional balance. However, **there are several reasons that led me to consider that food education for children, directly approached from a nutri-centric perspective, is neither coherent nor relevant.**

As I have also expressed before, learning about nutritional balance is relevant for health only if it is based on real and whole foods, but it is also less accessible, more technical, and more challenging to understand than the "real" dimension (see again Figure No. 1).

According to this logic, **starting by teaching different nutrients and what nutritional balance is would mean starting with the most difficult, but also potentially misleading children by making them think that eating healthily is primarily about meeting nutritional needs and maintaining a balanced diet.** Not only is this a false conception, but it could also do more harm than good, as **an approach that primarily or only focuses on nutritional balance may lead to eating anything and everything, including the most harmful foods, thinking that they are "healthy" because the carbohydrate, protein, and vitamin quantities on the packaging seem well "balanced."**[214]

And we saw this clearly in the presentation of the survey results. Nutritional balance in children's diets is not the most likely factor to lead to future social inequalities in health and the potential development of chronic diseases in the poorer population. Quite the opposite: disparities in food quality (mostly whole foods in affluent children and ultra-processed foods in disadvantaged children), variety (variations in the sizes of food repertoires and daily

---

[213] This stance involves criticizing the use of the term "nutritional quality," which involves the bias and oxymoron of conflating qualitative and quantitative dimensions.

[214] A food or product is never truly "balanced." Only a diet can be considered balanced. Moreover, the concept of balance is a debatable dimension subject to numerous discussions.

consumption habits), and additive intake are likely to be the causes of these disparities, not nutritional balance itself.

Therefore, if we want to implement food education at school with the aim of combating chronic diseases (including obesity) and social inequalities in health, **starting by teaching children about different nutrients, their roles, and the importance of a diet that balances them would likely serve almost no purpose!**

Nutritional balance remains, of course, a fundamental aspect of the links between nutrition and health, and **education about nutrients and balance will undoubtedly be essential, but only after acquiring the basics about what determines food quality**. It is, therefore, challenging to envisage this for children from kindergarten to elementary school, but it could theoretically be possible, provided that food education at school becomes such an important measure that enough time is dedicated to respecting a coherent chronology of the various learnings it requires. I strongly doubt that this will happen in the near future (at least in France).

In a more realistic scenario, it would be much preferable to leave the learning of what nutrients are and what their roles are to secondary education, middle school, or high school, and thus to adolescents who have already been educated in elementary school with general and basic knowledge about food quality.

These considerations might suggest that I am defending a certain ideological position or taking sides in an intellectual war between advocates of "reductionist" (nutri-centric) and "holistic" (qualitative) conceptions of nutrition. However, I take the risk of raising the alarm and emphasizing this point because I sincerely believe it is a crucial issue for food education, which will have immensely important consequences on children's representations and practices.

I am even willing to bet that starting by educating children about nutrients and nutritional balance, without addressing the qualitative dimension first, will change almost nothing in the

prevalences of obesity, type-2 diabetes, cardiovascular diseases, and other nutrition-related chronic diseases, even if practiced for thirty years.

The main problem we will encounter here is that everything related to this conception of what determines food quality, including the degree of processing, food matrix, and matrix effect, corresponds to fairly **recent knowledge, and in that sense, it is a forward-looking position, even in 2024!** This is because researchers in nutrition have been focusing on nutrients for more than seventy years. It is only in the last fifteen years that we have started to delve a little more, sometimes marginally, into what prompted us to understand that food quality is more important than the quantity of nutrients.

As a result, entire careers of researchers have been built on a nutri-centric approach to the effects of food on health, and it will undoubtedly be very difficult (for them[215]) to agree with the proposition I am formulating. This is as true as it is easy to see that these researchers are the most established in the academic and political world, both in terms of influence and power, so they are the most likely to make decisions (if there is ever real progress for food education in schools one day).

In any case, I don't have too many illusions about what my work can (or cannot) achieve in terms of actions and concrete progress: I am simply presenting its fruits in their most sincere form, for the sake of thoroughness.

Beware of measures limited to improving school canteen meals

In addition, regarding what does not work and is not coherent in terms of food education in schools, I would like to **warn elected**

---

[215] What is also rationally understandable. When one invests more than twenty or thirty years of a career (and daily energy and time) in a certain direction or idea, it seems very difficult to be able to question them, regardless of the truthfulness of the criticisms one may face (which is called a commitment bias).

officials and local decision-makers about initiatives taken for healthier school meals.

It is true that I have not addressed this aspect much in this book, although it was probably expected by the readers. **Obviously, actions to improve the quality of meals served in school cafeterias are also very important for children's nutrition, especially since they can contribute, too, to combating social inequalities in health and chronic diseases.**

Indeed, sometimes, especially for some poor children, **the school canteen lunch may represent the opportunity to have the only healthy and complete meal of the day**. School meals are also, like taste class workshops, significant levers to introduce children to new foods and dishes, which they can then potentially request from their parents.

However, based on my experience in the field, **offering healthier school meals with higher-quality products is not only ineffective but also cannot be considered a food education measure if the initiative is not accompanied by real educational actions conducted outside the canteen.**

The problem of meal quality in school canteens is often, beyond knowledge and consideration gaps, linked to budget limitations. To be able to serve healthier and higher-quality meals, for example, with fresh, organic, or local products, communities generally need to receive subsidies granted by the state (in other words, funded by the money of the French[216]).

It seems implausible and unfair to me that taxpayers' money could be used to pay for more expensive meals, half of which end up in the trash. This is what is highly likely to happen if no educational

---

[216] In the case where school canteen meals maintain the same cost for parents but include higher-quality and more expensive products, requiring assistance from municipalities.

action is implemented outside the cafeteria (I observed this in the field).

It is, therefore, the duty of elected officials to always accompany such initiatives with food education measures that go beyond simply encouraging children to taste (in other words, take a small bite) the foods served during cafeteria meals or putting up posters on the walls.

One could also criticize the few solutions that I propose in terms of food education at school by emphasizing that if educational actions are not coupled with practice (especially during canteen meals), all of this serves absolutely no purpose. I fully understand this kind of argument, although I do not agree with it.

In my opinion, it is even better to limit it to theoretical education, which aims primarily to awaken children to the idea that there are important links between what they eat and their long-term health, rather than just introducing healthier school meals without educational efforts.

Of course, ideally, it is best to combine both types of action.

What is coherent and seems to work

These observations, drawn from both fieldwork and elements from literature and logical reasoning, have led me to try to go against what is not coherent and does not work. Thus, **a consistent food education, aiming at least to combat chronic diseases and social inequalities in health, must be anchored in a relevant consideration of the links between food and health and should move from the general, which also appears as the most important, to the specific.**

These two ideas ultimately converge somewhat. What I conceive as a "relevant consideration of the links between food and health" must systematically include the distinction between food quality and nutrient quantity. It is logical that if I took the risk and time to outline my own conception of what constitutes a healthy diet, it is because I judge it to be relevant.

It is true that I also developed this because I could not find a "system" regarding what a healthy diet is that fully corresponded to my thinking. Not because I want reality to match my thoughts, but rather because I am constantly trying to adapt the latter to the truth, based on the information and knowledge I confront daily.

Above all, it would be essential to ensure never to educate about food with ultra-processed products or through products that are not authentic[217] (whose matrices have been too degraded and contain additives)!

Furthermore, practical workshops like the taste class represent excellent opportunities to expand the food repertoires of children who sometimes have limited access to a variety of products outside of school. **It would be relevant to organize this type of experience by introducing only and exclusively real and whole foods that the educator will be able to present, explain their origins, where they come from, how they are produced, and, if possible, talk about some of their beneficial effects on the body and on health. However, this requires knowledge, for which teachers will probably need developed support.**

As for moving from the most general to the most specific, this also appears as an obvious step, and I won't need to argue much to defend this idea. **It would logically involve not starting with technical jargon about different types of nutrients but rather talking to children about things and foods they know, or in other**

---

[217] I have to admit that I fail to understand the purpose of introducing highly processed products during a taste class as part of a food education program (a phenomenon I have not only observed in my field investigation but also noted in instances I won't mention by name). One of the justifications seems to be that pleasure is an important dimension of food. Certainly, I understand that. But what does education have to do with it in this case? What is its purpose? Children already have ample opportunities to taste commercially marketed deleterious foods for pleasure outside of school.

words, things that can directly make sense to them while keeping in mind not to stray too far from the health dimension.

This can involve fairly simple discussions: like presenting a food, explaining where it comes from, how it is raised or how it grows, what its potential effects on the body are, positive or negative. Talking about the agri-food industry, farming, agriculture, breeding, what food processing is (and its ultra-processing), what the different stages and activities necessary for the production and marketing of a product are, etc.

It is, in fact, a general approach to nutrition, focusing on it in a comprehensive, broad way and thus with an openness to many questions (which can occasionally slightly exceed the health dimension), rather than in a reduced manner to more specific and closed aspects.

Addressing these general questions with children will allow them to develop a certain awareness that food, with all that it implies in terms of consumption, have concrete effects on human health, but also on living beings and the environment (for example, on the state and fertility of soils, or on biodiversity), and on livestock, agriculture, or production activities. And these are things that can quickly make a lot of sense to children by enabling them to make connections with a set of information that link to each other.

This general awareness is fundamental because it will enable them to want to explore further the effects of food, ultimately leading to a first form of coherent awareness. **The goal is for children to wonder about the consequences of their food consumption.**

It is also evident that aiming to develop in children a genuinely interested awareness of the effects of nutrition will have to involve stimulating activities, and it will be essential not to make them feel guilty about their tastes or habits. It is undeniable that any form of guilt-tripping cannot be effective in making them interested in considering the effects of their food consumption on their health, also because they cannot be entirely masters of their daily food choices, which still depend primarily on decisions made by their parents.

Not making them feel guilty does not mean encouraging or praising their practices from a relativistic perspective that would claim "there's good everywhere," but rather attempting to maintain the most explanatory approach possible. Food education for health will always involve the risk that some children may understand that their daily practices are not healthy and, thus, in a resistant or rejecting approach, lose interest in what is being taught. The key is precisely to try to minimize this type of reaction as much as possible!

To reduce the risk that children do not become interested in what is being discussed with them, due to a disconnect between the educator's discourse and the reality experienced by the children, I concluded that the best approach would be to involve the children, for example, by inviting them to express themselves about what they experience and know. **This is also where a general, qualitative, and holistic approach to nutrition represents an advantage**.

The openness and multiplicity of topics it implies will allow children to express themselves and mobilize their own knowledge and representations of what concerns nutrition and the links between food and health. It is true that all of this can still seem a bit vague and too theoretical, which is why I will provide concrete examples of experiments I have conducted based on these reflections.

In the meantime, this part of the research has identified what is not coherent and does not work in food education at school and, based on this (and fieldwork), has grasped what is coherent and seems to work. That is, **starting from the general to the specific and thus beginning, from elementary school onwards, with a general, qualitative, and holistic approach to nutrition that will awaken awareness of the links between food and health; using participatory and explanatory methods; as well as ensuring not to stray too far from the health dimension, systematically anchoring**

it in a relevant consideration of the links between food and health (for example, during practical workshops, such as cooking or taste classes). Figure No. 3 summarizes the formulation of these three principles.

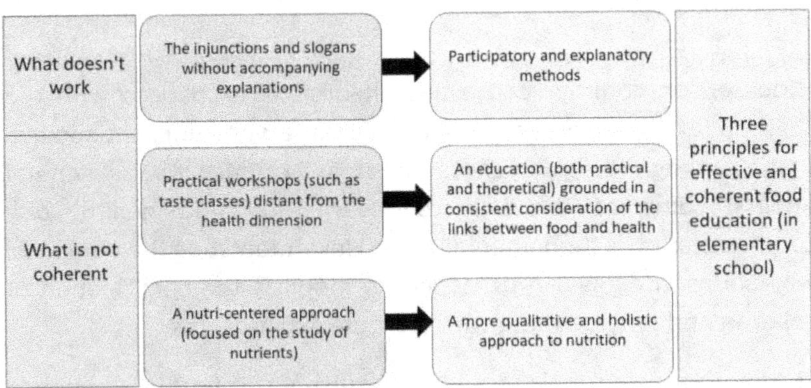

Figure No. 3: Food education at elementary school, from what doesn't work or isn't coherent to what is coherent and appears to work

This entire process would, of course, have very little interest if I had contented myself with these few theoretical abstractions, which perhaps do not mean much in concrete terms for the reader. Also, the developed ideas cannot truly have any value until they have been put into practice in the field and confronted with reality. It would also be naive to expect anything from a state institution or others for the implementation of direct actions taking into account my work.

Be that as it may, I decided to conduct my own experiments to test the validity of these theories, with my own means, albeit modest (see very limited), but still better than nothing. Having already obtained the necessary authorizations to conduct a sociological survey in four schools, I proposed to conduct interviews again, but this time collectively[218], with entire classes. I took this opportunity

---

[218] These collective interviews provided an opportunity to ask the children some more sociological questions (similarly to what I did during the semi-structured interviews) and to introduce a few tests, the experience of which I describe here. As for the sociological questions posed prior to the experiments, most of their

to try to put into practice the three principles outlined above and observe the reactions of the children.

Experimentation of a pedagogical method for food education at elementary school, derived from my work

I focused on communicative and theoretical exchanges with the children (excluding practical taste or cooking workshops). It appears that, aiming for awareness and awakening to a general understanding of the links between food and health, oral communication is fundamental and no less interesting than practical workshops. It allows, in particular, to mobilize the participation of children and provide them with multiple explanations.

The method used is illustrated in Figure No. 4 (and is ultimately nothing magical):

results remain very similar to what I have presented so far (which is why I will not go into detail about them).

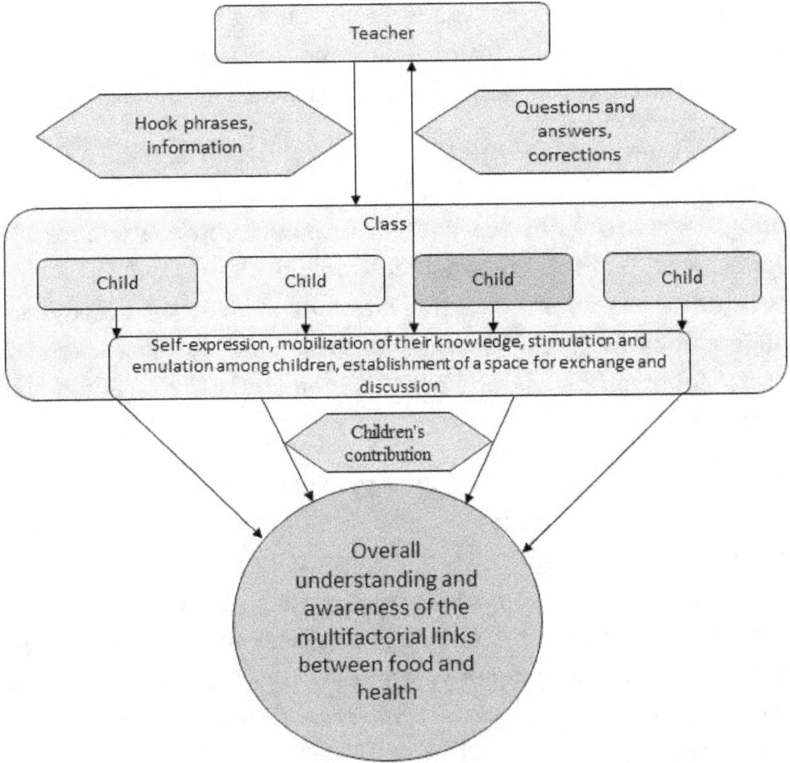

Figure No. 4: Participatory and explanatory food education method tested in the field ("holistic food education")

I named this method "holistic food education" because it intentionally aims to be broad and general rather than specific or focused on a particular aspect, seeking a multifactorial understanding of the links between food and health.

This method involves introducing attention-grabbing statements to children, such as quotes, that are accessible to them in terms of both formulation and substance. Subsequently, they are asked to express their thoughts on these statements, creating a discussion around general topics that contribute to their awareness of the connections between food and health. **This method has the advantage of directly giving children a voice to maximize not only their attention and engagement but also to avoid dictating information that might**

not interest them. Similarly, addressing general topics allows for a holistic approach to nutrition, with the possibility of mobilizing multiple ideas and touching on various issues.

I used, as examples, the quote from Heraclitus: "The health of man is a reflection of the health of the earth"; Ludwig Feuerbach's quote: "We are what we eat"; the maxim often attributed to Hippocrates: "Let food be thy medicine"; or the remarks of a child collected during a semi-directive interview: "If you have a cow and you feed it badly, it will be sick, and it will make you sick when you eat it," followed by asking how this idea could similarly apply to plants and fruits.

These statements allowed children to express themselves on broad and open-ended questions, establishing conversations that I sometimes redirected towards food, without restricting their expression. **It became apparent that disadvantaged children, who seemed mostly disinterested in topics related to the links between food and health in previous semi-directive interviews, became highly engaged in these discussions once they could become true participants.**

In Box No. 5, there is an excerpt from a recorded exchange in a 5th-grade class at School A, with the participation of several children (I tried to involve as many as possible). After discussing the previously mentioned example about a "poorly fed" cow being "sick" and "making you sick when you eat it," I asked the children if "the cow" could be replaced by an apple.

"- Oh yes! If the apple can grow badly!

- If there are worms that get into the apples, the apple becomes rotten and expired.

- Apples grow on a tree. But then, if we mistreat the cow, it's like mistreating the tree, and then the apple is bad?

- (I steer the discussion) Does anyone have an idea of how we could mistreat an apple?

- Rip it off, throw it on the ground, and step on it.

And spit on it (the children laugh).

- Well, if we cut the apple tree. For example, if you cut the banana tree...

- In essence, it's like us... if you cut the apple tree, the apple will start to rot. And it's the same for the cow, when it's mistreated, well, its blood starts to... because of the nutrition, it lacks things in its body because of viruses, which can make it die...

- (I intervene again) So you see, it's interesting because you find a lot of common points between animals and fruits. So yes, a rotten apple is not good for us. And in what other cases can an apple be bad for us?

- Peeing on it.

- Putting toxic products...

- Oh yes! There are products to remove insects on apples... insecticides and pesticides, I believe.

- It's like if we put Coca-Cola to make it grow... because there are toxic things in Coca-Cola.

- (I steer the conversation back to the fact that the children managed to talk about toxic products.) You're talking to me about toxic products, can someone elaborate a bit? Someone I haven't heard much.

- It's chemistry... potions...

- There are insecticides, they are chemical products to kill insects, and it's also toxic.

- Some people wax apples with chemical products to show that they are much cleaner or prettier, except that it's bad, and you can also catch diseases because of that and die.

- Pesticides are like insecticides, it's like, for example, if you have vegetables in your garden and there are slugs or snails, it can kill them too, precisely. And I think it's not very good if you eat them after the vegetables.

- I have a question, can you make pesticides with chemicals but also with natural things?

- (I respond) So, we can prevent insects from invading fruits and vegetables naturally, yes. But everything that is chemical, scientists increasingly realize that it affects the human body and makes it sick in the long run.

- But there are people who say that, for example, organic is not necessarily better for health.

- (I bring it back) What is an organic food?

- Organic is like natural, for example, if an apple grows on a tree, we pick it and eat it directly, that's organic, in fact, there are no pesticides that have been put on the apples.

- Well, if there are no pesticides, it's definitely better then! [...]"

(Children from a 5th-grade class at School A).

This kind of discussion might seem somewhat anecdotal. However, I think that is not the case at all. **These same children, during the semi-directive interviews, never mentioned ideas like this (especially regarding organic and pesticides) and have never been so engaged in the conversation.** Their enthusiasm in the 4th and 5th-grade classes of Schools A and B was such that at the end of the session, the children kept asking their teachers if they were going to talk about nutrition in class and if they were going to review the topics we had discussed.

Although my interpretation may be somewhat biased, in the sense that the stimulation of the children may also have been partly caused by my presence as an external speaker at the school and outside their daily routine[219]. It seems, nonetheless, that giving children a voice in the context of food education is much more effective and interesting, yielding results, than dictating knowledge in a purely vertical manner.

Also, each child has been able to, in a way, contribute to the discussion and thus raise a particular factor of the multifactorial dimension that constitutes the links between human health, food, and the environment (as a condition of our health in the current context of the growth of chronic diseases).

As another example, in reaction to the previously mentioned Heraclitus quote, children from School B came up with ideas that "trees and plants help us breathe better," that "plants need bees to live, so we need bees," so that "bees are important, if we pollute too much, they die," then that "grass is also important because there are herbivorous animals," as well as "the earth is like our body, if we take care of it, we can live well." The mention of bees then prompted children to talk about honey, as the "sugar that doesn't expire," and then to ask, "why can honey help be less sick sometimes?"

I want to be clear here: **the approach I describe is not about advocating a certain relativism that would amount to thinking that making children say anything and everything can be useful anyway. The educator must also play a role as a guide and organizer for the development of reflection through discussion, sometimes redirecting it towards the links between food and health if necessary**. This requires having basic fundamental knowledge oneself, as an educator, also because this type of

---

[219] Nevertheless, it is important to consider the difference between semi-structured interviews, which are conducted individually, with an attempt not to influence the responses of the interviewees, and this type of experimentation, where the goal was precisely to stimulate the children.

exchange strongly arouses the curiosity of children, leading them to ask many questions.

This method does not claim to revolutionize food education, let alone to impose itself as a model to be systematically followed to practice it. This would be quickly limited in the case where food education classes are regularly given since the method presented is more of a way to introduce children to the idea that there are links between their food and their health, aiming for awareness (although it can be renewed over several sessions by addressing different themes).

It is simply about showing that it is neither wizardry nor complicated to develop coherent and functional approaches[220], once we have identified what does not work and is not consistent and to put them into practice in the field. The possibilities for forms of food education are, of course, numerous and relatively open to the creativity of educators, provided they fit well within the three principles presented earlier.

Conclusion of my contribution regarding food education at school

"The holistic food education" as a pedagogical method is rather recommended considering the current context in France and several countries: assuming there is no national food education program that is mandatory to provide and common to all public schools, and

---

[220] It might seem presumptuous to assert that this method is functional, in the sense that it is only a small-scale experimentation and would likely require a genuine evaluation process of the evolution of children's perceptions and behaviors over the long term to learn more about its effectiveness. However, pragmatism is also necessary: in the field, I observed what doesn't work with children and what is not coherent. I also witnessed their reactions during my tests, where it was quite surprising to note their sudden and intense interest in the subject (which does not seem to be gained so easily). Similarly, many exchanges I had with various stakeholders in food education supported these conclusions.

that initiatives must come from the will of teachers, associations, or communities.

This approach has been designed and tested at the elementary school level to be effective for all children, including the most disadvantaged, who are often the ones most in need of food education for health. It is likely that it would find its place at the beginning of middle school[221], but other methods will surely need to be considered for older adolescents, for whom the examples I provided are too simplistic, although the form of the method can still be relevant.

However, I think that my ideas about "what does not work and is not consistent" and "what works and seems to be consistent" have a more universal purpose and can be fully considered and taken into account when implementing food education or prevention approaches for any audience.

Participatory methods indeed offer many advantages. The fact is that nutrition is not just something that students will learn in class and that will, as knowledge, stay in the classroom, but a daily practice and a central part of individuals' lives (unlike mathematical operations or historical-geographical knowledge, often learned by adolescents only to get good grades on tests or exams, before eventually forgetting most of it). The developed explanations and participation allow better understanding and a more intense investment in knowledge acquisition, which is fundamental at any age.

Once again, if theoretical education (through communication), which I have mainly addressed here, can be coupled with practical

---

[221] Regarding this, see the article that we co-wrote with Alexandra Pech (who worked on her doctoral thesis on food education in secondary school) and with whom we arrived at some similar findings and conclusions: Pech A. & Lebredonchel L., Fardet A. (2023). Regards croisés sur l'éducation alimentaire. *Éducation, santé, sociétés*, Vol.9, No.2. https://doi.org/10.17184/eac.7724

actions (for example, through initiatives for healthier school meals or during cooking sessions), it is certainly even better.

Independent initiatives will probably be limited in their ability to have long-term effects compared to the benefits for society as a whole that a real centralized food education program could have but are crucial as they represent changes from the grassroots.

The lingering question remains: when will the French and other governments decide to build and enforce a true national food education program, according to a curriculum, from elementary school to high school (or at least middle school)? Unfortunately, because it will probably not happen tomorrow, this would be the most conducive solution to lead citizens toward healthier food representations and behaviors, surely contributing to better population health over time. The goal of writing this work had, among its main objectives, to demonstrate the urgency of its implementation.

Chapter 9: Messages to parents and people, for small changes from the bottom

I am well aware of the many limitations regarding this presentation of food education at school. Partly because it seems evident that it is high time to implement such initiatives in schools, not only to better combat obesity and various chronic diseases, but also for overall better health. Moreover, this decision belongs to the elected officials, and citizens, at their scale, can do little concrete in this regard.

For parents and all individuals, the first step toward potential changes from the bottom, of course, be the realization that the food they provide to their children and themselves plays a crucial role in maintaining good health or, conversely, in its long-term degradation.

In a liberal food market like ours, it comes down **to understand that most agro-food companies care little about the consequences their products may have on your health! The main goal is to make a profit!** For this, any marketing strategy is good, including the most perverse ones, such as attributing positive health effects to products that are, in fact, time bombs for chronic diseases.

Changes from the bottom will inevitably require widespread citizen awareness of the considerable dangers posed by ultra-processed foods, intensive agriculture and farming, various additives (especially when they multiply within a single product), **and everything artificially introduced and added to food for commercial and profit purposes.**

What I presented as the "real" dimension of food and the idea that quality is more important than nutrient quantity for health are unfortunately poorly known facts. While research is advancing in this direction, public authorities communicate too little on this subject with citizens. Awareness and the dissemination of this knowledge are no less crucial in addressing issues than food education at school. I also applaud the few researchers and practitioners working hard to popularize and make accessible all knowledge related to this topic.

In our current context of increasing chronic diseases, a liberal food market, and the normalization of ultra-processing[222], a trend that has continued for about sixty years, **it seems entirely fait to strongly recommend being more vigilant, if not highly suspicious, about what we ingest and give to children.** As politically incorrect as this idea may seem, it appears to be highly reasonable: **we are dealing with over-the-counter products that we deliberately know are BAD for health in multiple ways, without any regulation or taxation**[223] **imposed by the government.**

Companies selling such products will not pay any money or compensation to future chronic patients, who will have only their tears to shed and sometimes their entire lives ruined.

Times have changed: throughout history, our survival as humans depended on our ability to hunt (and gather), then largely on farming and agriculture, for **our current life to now depend on our ability to make coherent consumption choices related to the functioning of our bodies. This includes avoiding the many traps set within supermarket shelves.**

Of course, chronic diseases are not solely caused or prevented by diet. However, in an era where these diseases are growing and affecting more and more of our loved ones, it is nonsensical not to undertake major changes in how we consume and eat, especially

---

[222] Once again, eating real and whole foods is not the sole dimension of a diet beneficial to human health. However, it is consistent to think that the complete cessation of ultra-processed foods, on a national or global scale, would significantly reduce the prevalence of diet-related chronic diseases.

[223] Several researchers are opposed to measures such as taxing ultra-processed products, arguing that it would "discriminate against the poorest," given that they are the ones who consume them the most. However, in my opinion, this either stems from bad faith, or a perception of a "cultural whole," without realizing that reality is not solely composed of the social aspect, but also involves health issues.

when we know how much of a double-edged sword food can be concerning health.

I address directly the disadvantaged, deprived, or commonly referred to as the lower strata of society. Whether you work or not, whether you wake up every morning at dawn to engage in alienating activities you have no desire to undertake, only to return home exhausted and pursued by all the problems that poverty can bring: I know how important your children are to you, and how much hope you have for them to be able, later on, to break free from the conditions that are yours, and to break the chains of poverty.

Be well aware that the daily foods you provide to your children will constitute a significant part of the fuel necessary for their social ascension. Consequently, and aware of this, **it is extremely difficult to rise socially, educate oneself, pursue studies, and escape poverty when one is in poor health or chronically ill.** I understand that, with all the difficulties life imposes on you, the essential thing for you is to see your children smile. It is true that, when resources are limited, this can involve "pleasures" that are affordable and accessible.

However, you must be much more cautious about what you give to your children and the advertisements that influence their tastes and desires, because the current consumption market is like a real jungle, where profit is the king. Take more interest in the products you buy, read their labels. If these labels often contain more than five ingredients and several additives, you are dealing with poor-quality ultra-processed foods or pieces of foods combined together that have lost most of their energy quality, accompanied by chemical cocktails. These products have every chance of being harmful to your children's health, and their daily consumption implies a high risk of contributing to making them sick one day. I am not here to preach, and I have no lessons to give to anyone. However, **it is important that you know what you are doing and the consequences it may have.**

It is also a reality: a child's smile caused by false tastes – artificial and optimized for instant pleasure and significant dopamine secretion, encouraging overconsumption while disrupting satiety – is absolutely not a winner in the face of the effects it will have in the long term, as **the smile will probably not last long**.

Especially since it is very likely that this "pleasure" associated with these products, however significant it may be judged, is caused by neuro-gustatory mechanisms as well as the social and affective aspect it touches. That's why advertising campaigns for ultra-processed foods targeting children always play on symbols related to what is popular among peer groups in the targeted age range.

As Valérie-Inès de la Ville pointed out, "*food is consumed for what it represents, what it allows in terms of social interactions with peers and the autonomy it provides to the child*," as well as for its "*playful*" dimension[224].

Marketing for this type of food targeting children does not hesitate to manipulate symbols to enrich companies at the expense of public health. Consuming them means accepting to be an easy prey, making oneself and one's children vulnerable. **It is also exchanging a few moments of "pleasure" for a potential life of illnesses.**

It can be argued again that low-income households "have no choice" but to consume ultra-processed foods daily, the cost of which is often cheaper than real food. Not only does this deterministic and victimization-prone posture have no chance of changing things (either accepting that the poorest make themselves sick or highly underestimating the harmful effects of daily ultra-processed consumption), **but I also do not think it is accurate in reality**. While being conscious of the high cost that a healthy daily diet can sometimes reach, I will reiterate that the portion of the French budget dedicated to food has gradually decreased since the

---

[224] De La Ville V.I., Tartas V. (2008). Transformer la participation de l'enfant aux activités de consommation alimentaire. *Enfance* (Presses Universitaires de France), 2008/3 Vol. 60 | pages 299 à 307, https://doi.org/10.3917/enf.603.0299

mid-20th century, at the same time that the portion dedicated to medicines has increased.

It seems that technical and technological advances related to the industrialization of food, as well as the blind trust we tend to attribute to them, have somehow led to the belief that we could spend less on food to save and afford more expenses for other purchases (appliances, technology, clothing, etc.). It will now be essential to realize that we need to be much more cautious about industrial food, whose ultra-processing, which was not well known and understood twenty years ago, and of which we have almost no hindsight. In any case, the savings made on the consumption of lower-quality food, especially those that are no longer real, do not constitute a beneficial calculation in terms of gains and losses, especially in the long term.

Indeed, it is much more interesting, concerning calculation, to devote a little more of one's budget to food and contribute to optimizing one's chances of staying healthy, even if it means restricting one's consumption of planned obsolescence technological devices or industrial clothes that will no longer be worn after a year or two, rather than saving on food and maintaining the probability that one's body will develop a chronic disease over the next fifteen years.

Life is relatively short, and despite what transhumanists think, erroneously believing that the human body is made of replaceable parts like the spare parts of a car, we have only one organism![225] And its degradation, which can be a very rapid process, is often irreversible and condemns us for the rest of our lives.

It is not specifically the poor who are invited here to spend a little more on food and spend less elsewhere, but the entire population (although it is much easier and less constraining when you are rich).

---

[225] Which entirety does not equate to the sum of its parts.

When we consume junk food, we encourage and invest in large agro-food companies that have only one goal: to enrich themselves, without any ethics and without the slightest concern for public health. We also contribute to the normalization of this kind of practice. In view of the significant health issues of real and whole foods versus the ultra-processing industry, it is essential to encourage small producers, farmers, and breeders who focus on quality. This necessarily involves a revaluation of food as a primary consumer good for life. In other words, we would probably need to be willing to pay a little more[226] for our food to live better and to break free from the infernal cycle into which hyper-industrialization of food has led us for more than a century.

For over sixty years, we have been spending less and less on food, losing in quality, gradually enriching multinationals while farmers and small producers commit suicide[227]. It is time to question ourselves and realize **that this societal model is a resounding failure, in which we are increasingly obese, sick, consumers of medication, and deprived of our sovereignty in the ability to produce and feed ourselves locally.**

The merits of "resilience" and "food sovereignty" have recently been often mentioned and in vogue (in France), as well as the multiple advantages of local and ethical productions and consumptions towards producers: it is therefore essential to rethink the value of food. This surely implies being willing to pay a little more[228] for what truly deserves it (for those who can).

---

[226] This also does not mean going beyond one's means. This proposition is more to be understood as "putting a little more money into one's diet to put a little less into other less important things," similar to everything related to mass consumption (electronics, household items, etc.). Unfortunately, the context of super-inflation we are currently experiencing is not going to help move in this direction.

[227] This is undoubtedly a sign of a sick society, both figuratively and literally.

[228] And I am well aware of how this idea may seem disagreeable to some. In a certain way, money represents energy converted into value commonly accepted by society as a whole (when it is produced through daily labor, and not printed out of

Moreover, **the cost of a relatively healthy diet is not necessarily exorbitant, provided that one is sufficiently educated to make relevant choices and capable of assessing the benefits of what one consumes compared to what one spends.**

More specifically, if we review what represents, in broad terms, a healthy diet: **eating real and whole foods does not necessarily cost more than eating ultra-processed, provided you choose the products you buy wisely**[229]. Still, it mainly costs more time for purchasing and preparing meals. Eating varied and balanced also requires spending more time researching and selecting products, cooking, but does not inevitably cost more than eating the same thing all the time. It is especially and primarily the act of eating while avoiding ingesting pathogenic chemicals, consuming what is labeled organic, which always costs more. Pesticides, chemical fertilizers, and other pollutants are indeed vectors of chronic diseases and bad for human health, but the higher cost of organic food does not prevent you from eating real and whole foods based, varied, and balanced, which is already a very good foundation for a healthy and partly protective diet.

---

thin air or earned through speculation, i.e., the selling or gambling of this energy - though that is not the subject of this work). Paying a bit more for higher-quality food is putting one's energy to receive it in return: that is, a profitable and winning investment. Of course, provided one can afford it.

[229] One could argue that eating whole foods inevitably costs more than eating ultra-processed foods: "that's what science says." I am referring here to the concrete reality and possibilities when you are in a supermarket aisle. Not mathematical calculations based on what is already trending, published in research articles, and leading to this type of assertion.

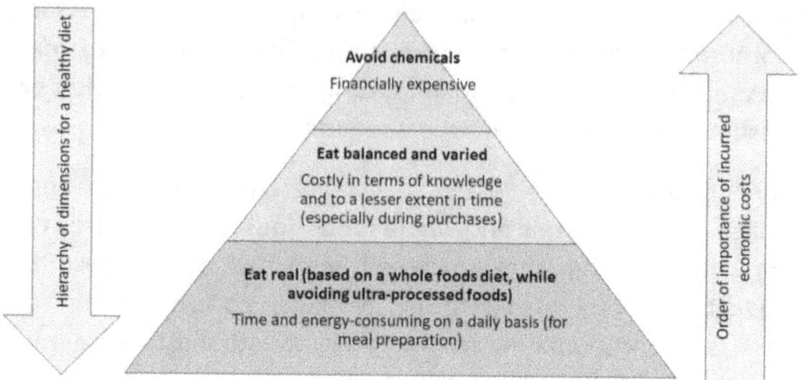

Figure No. 5: Constraints and importance of costs in different dimensions of a healthy diet

The main barriers to adopting a healthy diet seem to be more related to knowledge, time, and energy than to economic costs[230]. Conversely, energy is also partly acquired through this same healthy diet.

The time spent cooking can indeed be tedious and sometimes challenging to find, especially when family members have full-time jobs and return tired, often with many other things to take care of. **However, this is a beneficial investment, optimizing one's chances of gaining a lifetime of good health** (so that between twenty and forty minutes a day, which is certainly not insignificant, can, in return, help gain months or even years[231]).

---

[230] And my sociological research does not contradict this idea. It is not because, in general, there is a correlation between social position and the quality of nutrition (in terms of health) that one determines the other! Social position is also partly (not systematically) correlated with education, as it is very likely that the same trends I observed for social position are also true for the education and cultural capital of parents. (It is, in a way, a limitation of my research not to have delved further into the education and cultural capital of parents, but it must be considered that these cannot solely be reduced to the highest obtained diploma, and are thus particularly difficult to assess objectively and meaningfully.)

[231] While it is not always guaranteed... This is also a difficulty related to investing time and energy in cooking whole foods every day: one may feel that a lot of oneself is put into it without being assured of good health (as many other factors can

In other words, increased consumption of ultra-processed foods may contribute to a certain "gain" of time in the short term on a daily basis, but comes with a high probability of losing years in terms of a healthy lifetime in the long run. On the other hand, a whole foods based diet involves spending time cooking daily, which may be considered a "loss" of time in the short term, but improves the chances of gaining a lifetime of good health in the long term.

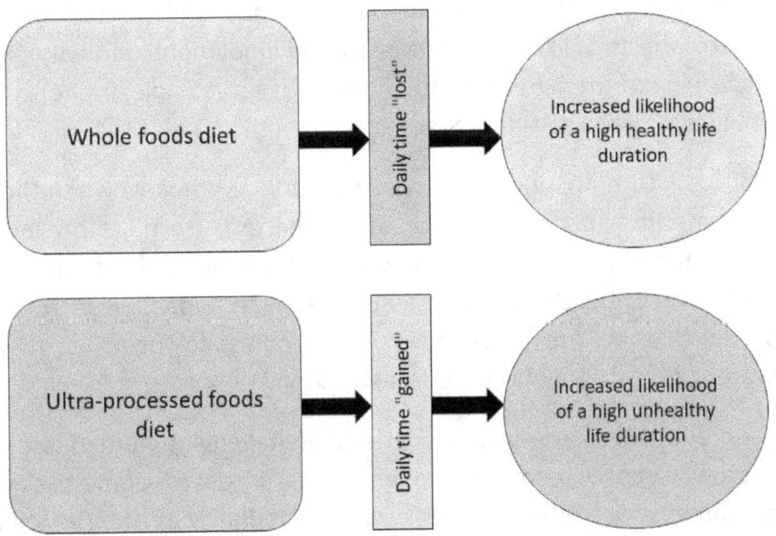

Figure No. 6: Whole Foods diet vs. ultra-Processed foods diet (and pre-prepared): short-term and long-term considerations of "gains" and "losses" in time

I could propose exactly the same argumentation regarding energy, although it is a bit more abstract and less objectively measurable with the means available to us currently.

In the extension of this reasoning, **it is about preferring to optimize one's chances of a long-term life through daily effort**s (which are not the end of the world, but can sometimes be challenging and

---

contribute to illnesses). Conversely, starting with a defeatist attitude from the outset is unlikely to help you maintain good health in the long run.

constraining when accustomed to pre-prepared products), **rather than an illusion of immediate comfort that will certainly cause discomfort for the rest of our lives**. In other words, choosing well-being (long-lasting) over "pleasure"[232] (instantaneous) and chronic discomfort.

We return to a problem previously discussed in a different formulation. I am conscious that one cannot rationally convince someone to prioritize their well-being despite their "pleasure" or certain aspects of immediate comfort and enjoyment. Similarly, the functioning of the human mind and body is too complex to hope to convince it not to self-destruct.

And this is something we commonly observe in smokers when they are sometimes perfectly aware of the harm they inflict on their bodies, but seem to feel they have no choice but to continue this practice that releases pleasure associated with dopamine secretion to which they are addicted, which seems to override their awareness of their delayed self-destruction.

Faced with these complex and ethically challenging human issues that are not easily resolved through theory, we always come back to the importance of the child, so that **the possibility of deteriorating one's own health as an adult remains somewhat debatable, but sabotaging the lives of children is not**. The latter is the very symbol of hope and the promise of a future, that absolutely needs to be nurtured by feeding them properly—it is our greatest responsibility.

In this sense, the idea of an "imperative of responsibility," as conceived by the philosopher Hans Jonas, is directly applicable to food and food education. This is also true for these words from the same man:

---

[232] I emphasize the use of quotation marks around the word "pleasure". The so-called pleasure associated with fake foods, promoted in advertising campaigns and by the well-intentioned who dare not condemn their consumption, is absolutely unappealing to a palate and an organism accustomed to the exclusive ingestion of real and whole foods.

"Kant's categorical imperative stated: 'Act in such a way that you can also will that your maxim becomes a universal law.' [...] An imperative adapted to the new type of human action and addressing the new type of subject of action would be formulated somewhat like this: 'Act in such a way that the effects of your action are compatible with the permanence of an authentically human life on earth'; or to express it negatively: 'Act in such a way that the effects of your action are not destructive to the future possibility of such a life.'"[233]

In a context where food can contribute to optimizing or compromising our future[234] and that of children, eating healthily and doing everything to ensure that children can learn to eat healthily, thus appears as a new "categorical imperative."

---

[233] Jonas H. (1979). *Le principe responsabilité, une éthique pour la civilisation technologique*. Traduit de l'allemand par Jean Greisch, Paris, Les Éditions du Cerf, 1990 (traduit de : *Das Prinzip Verantwortung*).

[234] Beyond poor health and chronic diseases, there is also the question of the future of human fertility, also linked to diet (and the endocrine disruptors it may contain).

Conclusion

This work has presented over six years of research, striving to make its understanding accessible while avoiding too much loss in precision and complexity. I have attempted to demonstrate how tastes, consumption habits, and representations of food vary among children and according to their social backgrounds, as they internalize food habitus that have varied effects on health.

Although speculative, **it is highly probable that these food habitus observed in children reflect different relationships with food based on their "social class," which are not only true for children, but for the entire population**.

These different food habitus mean that, considering the cause-and-effect relationships between food and health, **the poor are more likely to be in bad health than those who are wealthier (or particularly educated)**. In other words, coming from poorer backgrounds increases the likelihood of having a set of representations and tastes that lead to dietary practices likely to result in long-term health issues.

I did not intend to present this social reality to denounce injustices or accuse the poor, but rather to share the findings of my work and shed light on what all of this implies in terms of societal issues and potentially the invisible (because long-term and difficult to measure) construction of what is commonly referred to as social inequalities in health.

It is evident that repeating daily behaviors conducive to the development of multiple health problems—such as a highly increased consumption of ultra-processed foods and meals purchased from fast-food restaurants, a diet lacking in whole foods, fruits, vegetables, and quality animal products, as well as being low in variety and containing numerous additives—includes a strong probability of ending up in bad health.

Wanting to change this reality does not require asking the poor to emulate the wealthier or adopting a moralistic tone toward them. It seems entirely possible, although undoubtedly challenging, energy-consuming, and sometimes more expensive, to adapt one's tastes to a diet that is more real and whole foods based, varied, or even to try to avoid exposure to chemical pathogens, regardless of their origin (social, "ethnic," national, etc.).

This possibility requires an essential learning about the links between food and health, the knowledge of which, currently acquired through personal initiatives, is unsurprisingly much more developed among the wealthier than among the poor.

I have thus focused on food education as the most coherent and logical mean to address these issues. The part of my research dedicated to food education at school is rather additional and complementary, so this contribution is not as extensive as what I have produced in the sociology of food. It is certainly not easy and hardly possible to do everything oneself, although my reflections, analyses, and proposals on this subject stem from a pragmatic willingness to go all the way, and they will probably be useful for any action to implement food education at school, on a small or large scale.

I would also be very happy to work on a genuine food education program at the primary or secondary school level, building on some of the aspects developed here. However, this would require resources beyond my individual capacity and over which I have no direct control, if we want something to be deployed on a large scale.

This is the main limitation of food education at school, as it remains a top-down solution that largely depends on the consideration given to it by decision-makers, or on smaller scales, by community movements, associations, or teachers, although smaller actions are often the most difficult and constraining to implement.

Beyond an explanation of what I mean by being "conscious of the links between food and health," which I consider necessary for interpreting the results of the sociological survey, the part dedicated to what I conceive as a healthy diet is also part of a pragmatic approach. Although I do not provide explicitly practical examples of a healthy daily diet (which is not the purpose of the work but can be easily deduced from the presented reasoning), **I hope readers can still find some interest and utility in enriching their knowledge and perhaps adapting their own diet or that of their children, for small changes from the bottom**.

The matrix effect and the order of importance between the degree of transformation and nutritional balance are still somewhat poorly understood questions. That is also why I decided to write this chapter, attempting to offer a coherent and accessible vision of what constitutes a healthy diet, taking into account as many essential parameters as possible, without overly complicating matters.

As mentioned in the brief biographical passage at the beginning of the book, I also allowed myself to write this part in opposition to what I call the hyperspecialization of sciences. Working hard to obtain a doctorate in an academic discipline does not require looking at the world through a single lens or observing only one dimension of reality. In this sense, **the matrix effect of foods is comparable to the division of labor and this hyperspecialization of sciences**. The more nutrients are isolated from their matrix, the more they deteriorate and lose nutritional and energetic quality. The more a worker performs a specific and specialized task, the more it becomes alienating and devoid of meaning. Similarly, the more science specializes and limits itself to the interest of a microcosm of knowledge, the more it risks losing relevance and utility, as well as the richness of thought. Unfortunately, the taste for "wholeness" (which corresponds to what philosophy used to be, before undergoing this organic process of division) seems as outdated as it is perilous nowadays. By confining myself in this book to a "sociology of food, conscious of the links between food and health," I am ready to assume this choice and remain open to debate. End of the aside; I now return to the stakes of the presented research results.

In an increasingly unhealthy society, changes are and will inevitably be necessary regarding how we eat. **However, these changes cannot take place without awareness, and that is the main purpose of this book.** Sociology also has the interest, when made accessible to the entire society, of allowing us **to understand that concerns or situations we thought were personal are actually part of the logic of a social reality, where individuals are often unconsciously surpassed as such and not easily able to escape it.**

It is not easily demonstrable, "scientifically" and with directly mobilizable referenced evidence, that the poorest are the most chronically ill specifically due to their diet (chronic diseases, again, result from a plurality of factors). However, I highlight the fact that it remains very probable that there are significant links between the two.

Understanding that one's own condition is not exclusive to one's individual self, but corresponds to a reality that surpasses us as individuals constitutes a driving force for the possibility of change.

If you come from a precarious background, grew up eating ultra-processed foods daily, had an unhealthy diet according to other parameters explained earlier, and are in poor health[235]: it is surely not a result of chance. **Becoming aware of this condition can be a first step to prevent your children from "inheriting"[236] this curse.**

---

[235] I know a few people over thirty who are in this situation, and I don't think they are isolated cases. Once again, the scope of the sociological research that I have focused on children does not seem to be understood as limited to childhood, but rather as representing a mirror of a reality that extends to the entire society (to the future adults that children will become, as well as to the former children who are now adults).

[236] I think that many pathologies, which are still commonly attributed to genetic factors, actually depend on behaviors (or «interactions with the environment») that are similar between parents and children, transmitted through education. Recent discoveries in epigenetics support this idea: we now know that certain genes linked to diseases may not be 'activated' based on our practices and exposures. This is not to deny or minimize the influence of genetic factors, but to draw attention to the

Beyond a deliberately cliché title, this book and these ideas are, of course, not specifically addressed to the poor or the rich (especially since these terms remain relative and subjective) but to any curious mind that has already been interested, directly or indirectly, in food, its effects on health, or the fact that we do not eat the same things depending on where we come from.

Hoping that its reading has been enriching for you in one way or another, and thanking you sincerely for it, I do not wish you "good luck" but the possibility of making good choices, enjoying good food, and maintaining good health.

---

fact that it does not seem appropriate to reduce, at least as much as currently done, pathologies to genetic causes without first examining the lifestyles involved.

References

Aguilera J.M. (2018). The food matrix: implications in processing, nutrition and health. *Critical Reviews in Food Science and Nutrition*, 59(22), 3612–3629. https://doi.org/10.1080/10408398.2018.1502743

Alami F., Alizadeh M., Shateri K. (2022). The effect of a fruit-rich diet on liver biomarkers, insulin resistance, and lipid profile in patients with non-alcoholic fatty liver disease: a randomized clinical trial. *Scandinavian journal of gastroenterology*, 57(10), 1238–1249. https://doi.org/10.1080/00365521.2022.2071109

Alvarenga A., Bana e Costa C.A., Borrell C. et al. (2019. Scenarios for population health inequalities in 2030 in Europe: the EURO-HEALTHY project experience. *International Journal for Equity in Health*, 18, 100. https://doi.org/10.1186/s12939-019-1000-8

Anses. (2012). Disparités socio-économiques et apports alimentaires et nutritionnels des enfants et adolescents. Rapport d'étude, Paris, Anses.

Backett-Milburn K., Wills W., Roberts M.L., Lawton J. (2010). Food and family practices: teenagers, eating and domestic life in differing socio-economic circumstances. *Children's Geographies*, 8(3), 303-314. https://doi.org/10.1080/14733285.2010.494882

Beasley D.E., Koltz A.M., Lambert J.E., Fierer N., Dunn R.R. (2015). The Evolution of Stomach Acidity and Its Relevance to the Human Microbiome. *PLoS One*, 10(7): e0134116. https://doi.org/10.1371/journal.pone.0134116

Bjelakovic G., Nikolova D., Gluud C. (2014). Antioxidant supplements and mortality. *Current opinion in clinical nutrition and metabolic care,* 17(1), 40–44, https://doi.org/10.1097/MCO.0000000000000009

Bjelakovic G., Nikolova D., Gluud L.L., Simonetti R.G., Gluud C. (2012). Antioxidant supplements for prevention of mortality in healthy participants and patients with various diseases. *Cochrane Database of Systematic Reviews*, https://doi.org/10.1002/14651858.CD007176.pub2

Bjelakovic G., Nikolova D., Simonetti R.G., Gluud C. (2005). Antioxidant supplements for prevention of gastrointestinal cancers. *The Lancet*, Volume 365, Issue 9458, 471-472, https://doi.org/10.1016/S0140-6736(05)17858-1

Boirie Y., Dangin M., Gachon P. et al. (1997). Slow and fast dietary proteins differently modulate postprandial protein accretion. *Proceedings of the National Academy of Sciences*, 94(26): 14930-5. https://doi.org/10.1073/pnas.94.26.14930

Boltanski L. (1971), Les usages sociaux du corps. *Annales*, 26-1, 205-233

Bonnewitz, P. (2002). *Premières leçons sur la sociologie de Pierre Bourdieu*. Paris, Presses Universitaires de France.

Bourdieu P. (1979). *La Distinction : critique sociale du jugement*. Paris, Les Éditions de minuit.

Bourdieu P. (1994). *Raisons pratiques. Sur la théorie de l'action*. Paris, Éditions du Seuil.

Bourdieu P., Passeron J-C. (1970). *La Reproduction. Éléments pour une théorie du système d'enseignement*. Paris, Les Éditions de minuit.

Carbone J.W., Pasiakos S.M. (2019). Dietary Protein and Muscle Mass: Translating Science to Application and Health Benefit. *Nutrients*, 11(5), 1136. https://doi.org/10.3390/nu11051136

Chen X., Zhang Z., Yang H., Qiu P., Wang H., Wang F., Zhao Q., Fang J., Nie J. (2020). Consumption of ultra-processed foods and health outcomes: a systematic review of epidemiological studies. *Nutrition journal*, 19(1), 86, https://doi.org/10.1186/s12937-020-00604-1

Cicolella A. (2013). *Toxique planète, le scandale invisible des maladies chroniques*. Paris, Éditions du Seuil.

Ciuris C., Lynch H.M., Wharton C., Johnston C.S. (2019). A Comparison of Dietary Protein Digestibility, Based on DIAAS Scoring, in Vegetarian and Non-Vegetarian Athletes. *Nutrients*, 11(12):3016. https://doi.org/10.3390/nu11123016

Davidou S., Frank K., Christodoulou A., Fardet A. (2022). Organic food retailing: to what extent are foods processed and do they contain markers of ultra-processing ?. *International Journal of Food Sciences and Nutrition*, 73(2), p. 172-183. https://doi.org/10.1080/09637486.2021.1966395

De La Ville V.I., Tartas V. (2008). Transformer la participation de l'enfant aux activités de consommation alimentaire. *Enfance* (Presses Universitaires de France), 2008/3 Vol. 60 | pages 299 à 307, https://doi.org/10.3917/enf.603.0299

Devaux M., Sassi F. (2013). Social inequalities in obesity and overweight in 11 OECD countries. *European Journal of Public Health*, Volume 23, Issue 3, June 2013, Pages 464–469, https://doi.org/10.1093/eurpub/ckr058

Ditlevsen K., Halkier B., Holm L. (2022). Pathways of less healthy diets. An investigation of the everyday food practices of men and women in low income households. *Critical Public Health*, https://doi.org/10.1080/09581596.2022.2101917

Dozon J.P., Fassin D. (2001). *Critique de la santé publique*. Paris, Balland.

Drouard A. (2007). Perspectives historiques sur la notion de nutrition. Dans Audoin-Rouzea Frédérique et Sabban Françoise (dir), *Un aliment sain dans un corps sain – perspectives historiques*, Tours, Presses universitaires François Rabelais.

Fardet A. (2016). Do the physical structure and physicochemical characteristics of dietary fibers influence their health effects?. In: Hosseinian F, Oomah B.D., Campos-Vega R. *Dietary fibre functionality in food & nutraceuticals: From Plant to Gut*. John Wiley & Sons: Hoboken.

Fardet A. (2017). *Halte aux aliments ultra-transformés*. Vergèze, Thierry Soucard Éditions.

Fardet A. (2017). L'effet matrice des aliments, un nouveau concept. *Pratiques en nutrition*, n°52, http://doi.org/10.1016/j.pranut.2017.09.009

Fardet A. (2017). La classification NOVA : degré de transformation des aliments et santé. Université d'été de Nutrition, Centre de Recherche en Nutrition Humaine (CRNH). Clermont-Ferrand, France. ⟨hal-01697078⟩.

Fardet A. (2018). Choisir des aliments non transformés. *L'écologiste*, n°53, vol 19 n°3.

Fardet A., Lebredonchel L., Rock E. (2021). Empirico-inductive and/or hypothetico-deductive methods in food science and nutrition research: which one to favor for better global health?. *Critical Reviews in Food Science and Nutrition*, Taylor & Francis, 2021, p. 1-14. https://doi.org/10.1080/10408398.2021.1976101

Fardet A., Rock E. (2022). Chronic diseases are first associated with the degradation and artificialization of food matrices rather than with food composition: calorie quality matters more than calorie quantity. *European journal of nutrition*, 61(5), 2239–2253. https://doi.org/10.1007/s00394-021-02786-8

Fielding-Singh P. (2017). A taste of inequality: Food's symbolic value across the socioeconomic spectrum. *Sociological Science*, 4, 424. https://doi.org/10.15195/v4.a17

Fischler C. (1990). *L'Homnivore : Le goût, la cuisine et le corps*. Paris, Odile Jacob.

Gauthier R.F. (2014). *Ce que l'école devrait enseigner, pour une révolution de la politique scolaire en France*. Paris, Dunos.

Giampieri F., Forbes-Hernandez T.Y., Gasparrini M., Afrin S., Cianciosi D., Reboredo-Rodriguez P., Varela-Lopez A., Quiles J.L., Mezzetti B., Battino M. (2017). The healthy effects of strawberry bioactive compounds on molecular pathways related to chronic diseases. *Annals of the New York Academy of Sciences,* 1398(1), 62–71. https://doi.org/10.1111/nyas.13373

Glaser B.G., Strauss A.L. (1967). *The discovery of the grounded theory.* Chicago, Aldine.

Gojard S. (2000). L'alimentation dans la prime enfance, diffusion et réception des normes de puériculture. *Revue française de sociologie*, 41, 3, p. 475-512.

Gupta S., Hawk T., Aggarwal A., Drewnowski A. (2019). Characterizing ultra-processed foods by energy density, nutrient density, and cost. *Frontiers in Nutrition*, 6, 70, https://doi.org/10.3389/fnut.2019.00070

Haber G.B., Heaton K.W., Murphy D., Burroughs L.F. (1977). Depletion and disruption of dietary fibre. Effects on satiety, plasma-glucose, and serum-insulin. *Lancet* (London, England), 2(8040), 679–682. https://doi.org/10.1016/s0140-6736(77)90494-9

Herpin N., Verger D. (2008). *Consommation et modes de vie en France, Une approche économique et sociologique sur un demi-siècle*. Paris, La découverte.

Hung H.C., Joshipura K.J., Jiang R., Hu F.B., Hunter D., Smith-Warner S.A., Colditz G.A., Rosner B., Spiegelman D., Willett W.C. (2004). Fruit and vegetable intake and risk of major chronic disease. *Journal of the National Cancer Institute*, 96(21), 1577–1584. https://doi.org/10.1093/jnci/djh296

Jodelet D. (2003). *Les représentations sociales*. Paris, Presses Universitaires de France. https://doi.org/10.3917/puf.jodel.2003.01

Jonas H. (1979). *Le principe responsabilité, une éthique pour la civilisation technologique*. Traduit de l'allemand par Jean Greisch, Paris, Les Éditions du Cerf, 1990 (traduit de : *Das Prinzip Verantwortung*).

Julia C., Martinez L., Allès B., Touvier M., Hercberg S., Méjean C., Kesse-Guyot E. (2018). Contribution of ultra-processed foods in the diet of adults from the French NutriNet-Santé study. *Public Health Nutrition*, 21(1), 27–37. https://doi.org/10.1017/S1368980017001367

Kesse-Guyota E., Péneaua S., Méjeana C., Szabo de Edelenyia F., Galana P., Hercberg S., Laironc D. (2013). Profil des consommateurs de produits bio en France : premières données de l'Étude Nutrinet-Santé. *Innovations Agronomiques*, Volume 32.

Klobukowski J.A., Skibniewska K.A., Kowalski I.M. (2014). Calcium bioavailability from dairy products and its release from food by in vitro digestion. *Journal of Elementology*, 19(1):277-88, https://doi.org/10.5601/jelem.2014.19.1.436

Leahy D., Wright J. (2016). Governing food choices: A critical analysis of school food pedagogies and young people's responses in contemporary times. *Cambridge Journal of Education*, 46(2), 233-246. http://doi.org/10.1080/0305764X.2015.1118440

Lebredonchel L. Fardet A. (2022). How French children food representations and tastes vary according to their social backgrounds: a study of disparities in food habitus. *Health Sociology Review*, online publication https://doi.org/10.1080/14461242.2022.2148832

Lebredonchel L., Lemarchand F., Fardet A. (2022), « La sociologie de l'alimentation comme piste pour lutter contre les maladies chroniques et les inégalités sociales de santé ». *Natures Sciences Sociétés*, publication en ligne. https://doi.org/10.1051/nss/2022027

Leonard W.R., Roberton M.L. (1992). Nutritional Requirement and Human Evolution: a Bioenergetics Model. *American journal of human biology*, 4: 179-195. https://doi.org/10.1002/ajhb.1310040204

Lerner A. (2016). Multiple Food Additives Enhance Human Chronic Diseases. *SOJ Microbiology & Infectious Diseases*, 4. 01-02. https://doi.org/10.15226/sojmid/4/2/00149

Lescinsky H., Afshin A., Ashbaugh C., Bisignano C., Brauer M., Ferrara G., Hay S.I., He J., Iannucci V., Marczak L.B., McLaughlin S.A., Mullany E.C.,

Parent M.C., Serfes A.L., Sorensen R.J.D., Aravkin A.Y., Zheng P., Murray C.J.L. (2022). Health effects associated with consumption of unprocessed red meat: a Burden of Proof study. *Nature Medicine*, 28(10), 2075–2082. https://doi.org/10.1038/s41591-022-01968-z

Mallarino C., Gómez L.F., González-Zapata L., Cadena Y., Parra D.C. (2013). Advertising of ultra-processed foods and beverages: children as a vulnerable population. *Revista De Saude Publica*, 47 (5): 1006–1010. https://doi.org/10.1590/s0034-8910.2013047004319

Mariotti F., Gardner C.D. (2019). Dietary Protein and Amino Acids in Vegetarian Diets-A Review. *Nutrients*, 11(11), 2661. https://doi.org/10.3390/nu11112661

Marrón-Ponce J., Sánchez-Pimienta T., Louzada M.L.C., Batis C. (2018). Energy contribution of NOVA food groups and sociodemographic determinants of ultra-processed food consumption in the Mexican population. *Public health nutrition*, 21(1), 87–93. https://doi.org/10.1017/S1368980017002129

Martines R.M., Machado P.P, Neri D.A., Levy R.B., Rauber F. (2019). Association between watching TV whilst eating and children's consumption of ultraprocessed foods in United Kingdom. *Maternal & Child Nutrition*, 15 (4). e12819. https://doi.org/10.1111/mcn.12819

Maurice A. (2014). *Les préadolescents comme ressorts des actions de santé publique : Analyse d'un projet d'éducation alimentaire en collège*. [Thèse de doctorat, Université de Paris]. https://www.theses.fr/2014PA05H008

Monteiro C.A. et al. (2016). Food classification Public health, NOVA. The star shines bright. *World Nutrition*, Volume 7, Number 1, March 2016.

Murray C.J. (2012). Global Burden of Disease 2010: a multi-investigator collaboration for global comparative descriptive epidemiology. *The Lancet*, vol. 380/9859, p. 2055-2058. https://doi.org/10.1016/S0140-6736(12)62134-5

Omran A. (1971). The Epidemiological Transition: A Theory of the Epidemiology of Population Change. *The Milbank Memorial Fund Quarterly*, 49 (4), p. 509-538.

Oncini F. (2019). Feeding distinction: Economic and cultural capital in the making of food boundaries. *Poetics*, 73, 17-31. https://doi.org/10.1016/j.poetic.2019.02.002

Oncini F. (2019). Feeding distinction: Economic and cultural capital in the making of food boundaries. *Poetics*, 73, 17-31. https://doi.org/10.1016/j.poetic.2019.02.002

Oncini, F. (2020). Cuisine, health and table manners: Food boundaries and forms of distinction among primary school children. *Sociology*, 54(3), 626-642. https://doi.org/10.1177/0038038519880087

Ovied-Solís C.I., Cornejo-Manzo S., Murillo-Ortiz B.O., Guzmán-Barrón M.M., Ramírez-Emiliano J. (2018). Los polifenoles de la fresa disminuyen el estrés oxidativo en enfermedades crónicas [Strawberry polyphenols decrease oxidative stress in chronic diseases]. *Gaceta medica de Mexico*, 154(1), 80–86. https://doi.org/10.24875/GMM.17002759

Pagliai G., Dinu M., Madarena M.P., Bonaccio M., Iacoviello L., Sofi F. (2020). Consumption of ultra-processed foods and health status: a systematic review and meta-analysis. *British Journal of Nutrition*, 125, 308-318, https://doi.org/10.1017/S0007114520002688

Paula Neto H.A., Ausina P., Gomez L.S., Leandro J., Zancan P., Sola-Penna M. (2017). Effects of Food Additives on Immune Cells As Contributors to Body Weight Gain and Immune-Mediated Metabolic Dysregulation. *Frontiers in immunology*, 8, 1478. https://doi.org/10.3389/fimmu.2017.01478

Pech A. & Lebredonchel L., Fardet A. (2023). Regards croisés sur l'éducation alimentaire. *Éducation, santé, sociétés*, Vol.9, No.2. https://doi.org/10.17184/eac.7724

Phillips S.M. (2017). Current Concepts and Unresolved Questions in Dietary Protein Requirements and Supplements in Adults. *Frontiers in Nutrition*, 4. https://doi.org/10.3389/fnut.2017.00013

Régnier F., Masullo A. (2009). Obésité, goûts et consommation : Intégration des normes d'alimentation et appartenance sociale. *Revue française de sociologie*, 50, 747-773. https://doi.org/10.3917/rfs.504.0747

Robertson A., Lobstein T., Knai C. (2007), Obesity and socio-economic groups in Europe: evidence review and implications for action. Brussels: European Commission.

Savage J.S., Fisher J.O, Birch L.L. (2007). Parental influence on eating behavior: conception to adolescence. *The Journal of Law, Medicine & Ethics*, 35(1), 22-34. https://doi.org/10.1111/j.1748-720X.2007.00111.x

Scaglioni S., De Cosmi V., Ciappolino V., Parazzini F., Brambilla P., Agostoni C. (2018). Factors Influencing Children's Eating Behaviours. *Nutrients*, 10(6), 706. https://doi.org/10.3390/nu10060706

Schlienger J.L. (2022). Petite histoire de l'épidémiologie de l'Antiquité à nos jours. *Médecine des Maladies Métaboliques*, Volume 16, Issue 2, 2022, P. 191-199, ISSN 1957-2557, https://doi.org/10.1016/j.mmm.2021.11.006

Schnabel L., Kesse-Guyot E., Allès B., Touvier M., Srour B., Hercberg S., Buscail C., Julia C. (2019). Association Between Ultraprocessed Food Consumption and Risk of Mortality Among Middle-aged Adults in France. *JAMA internal medicine*, 179(4), 490–498. https://doi.org/10.1001/jamainternmed.2018.7289

Scrinis G. (2013). *Nutritionism - the science and politics of dietary advice*. Columbia University Press, New York.

Simões B., Barreto, S.M., Molina M., Luft V.C., Duncan B.B., Schmidt M.I., Benseñor I., Cardoso L.O., Levy R.B., Giatti L. (2018). Consumption of ultra-processed foods and socioeconomic position: a cross-sectional analysis of the Brazilian Longitudinal Study of Adult Health (ELSA-Brasil). *Cadernos de saude publica*, 34(3), e00019717. https://doi.org/10.1590/0102-311X00019717

Spiroux J. (2007). *Pathologies environnementales*. Paris, Éditions J.Lyon.

Trémolières J. (1971). *Qu'est-ce que la nutrition ?* Paris, Ronéo.

Vandevijvere S., Pedroni C., De Ridder K., Castetbon K. (2020). The cost of diets according to their caloric share of ultraprocessed and minimally processed foods in Belgium. *Nutrients*, 12, 9, 2787, https://doi.org/10.3390/nu12092787

Volpe S.L. (2019). Fruit and Vegetable Intake and Prevention of Chronic Disease. *ACSM's Health & Fitness Journal*, 5/6 2019, Volume 23, Issue 3, p 30-31. https://doi.org/10.1249/FIT.0000000000000474

Waddingham S., Shaw K., Van Dam P., Bettiol S. (2017). What motivates their food choice? Children are key informants. *Appetite*, 120, 514-522. https://doi.org/10.1016/j.appet.2017.09.029

World Economic Forum, Havard School of Public Health. (2011). The Global Economic Burden of Non-communicable Diseases.

World Health Organization. Global status report on non-communicable diseases 2010. April 2011.

9 7 9 8 8 7 8 6 4 3 3 2 0